GEOFFREY CHAUCER

Selected Poems

BLOOMSBURY
* POETRY *
CLASSICS

This selection by Ian Hamilton
First published 1999

Copyright © 1999 by Bloomsbury Publishing Plc

Bloomsbury Publishing Plc, 38 Soho Square,
London W1V 5DF

A CIP catalogue record for this book
is available from the British Library

ISBN 0 7475 4696 7

10 9 8 7 6 5 4 3 2 1

Typeset in Great Britain by
Hewer Text Limited, Edinburgh
Printed in Great Britain by St Edmundsbury Press, Suffolk
Jacket design by Jeff Fisher

CONTENTS

From THE CANTERBURY TALES

THE GENERAL PROLOGUE

Whan that Aprill with his shoures soote
The droghte of March hath perced to the roote,
And bathed every veyne in swich licour
Of which vertu engendred is the flour;
Whan Zephirus eek with his sweete breeth
Inspired hath in every holt and heeth
The tendre croppes, and the yonge sonne
Hath in the Ram his half cours yronne,
And smale foweles maken melodye,
That slepen al the nyght with open ye
(So priketh hem nature in hir corages),
Thanne longen folk to goon on pilgrimages,
And palmeres for to seken straunge strondes,
To ferne halwes, kowthe in sondry londes;
And specially from every shires ende
Of Engelond to Caunterbury they wende
The hooly blisful martir for to seke,
That hem hath holpen whan that they were seeke.
  Bifil that in that seson on a day,
In Southwerk at the Tabard as I lay
Redy to wenden on my pilgrymage
To Caunterbury with ful devout corage,
At nyght was come into that hostelrye
Wel nyne and twenty in a compaignye

Of sondry folk, by aventure yfalle
In felaweshipe, and pilgrimes were they alle,
That toward Caunterbury wolden ryde.
The chambres and the stables weren wyde,
And wel we weren esed atte beste.
And shortly, whan the sonne was to reste,
So hadde I spoken with hem everichon
That I was of hir felaweshipe anon,
And made forward erly for to ryse,
To take oure wey ther as I yow devyse.

THE PRIORESSE, THE KNIGHT AND THE SQUIRE

Ther was also a Nonne, a Prioresse,
That of hir smylyng was ful symple and coy;
Hire gretteste ooth was but by Seinte Loy;
And she was cleped madame Eglentyne.
Ful weel she soong the service dyvyne,
Entuned in hir nose ful semely;
And Frenssh she spak ful faire and fetisly,
After the scole of Stratford atte Bowe,
For Frenssh of Parys was to hire unknowe.
At mete wel ytaught was she with alle;
She leet no morsel from hir lippes falle,
Ne wette hir fyngres in hir sauce depe;
Wel koude she carie a morsel and wel kepe
That no drope ne fille upon hire brest.
In curteisie was set ful muchel hir lest.
Hir over-lippe wyped she so clene
That in hir coppe ther was no ferthyng sene
Of grece, whan she dronken hadde hir draughte.
Ful semely after hir mete she raughte.
And sikerly she was of greet desport,
And ful plesaunt, and amyable of port,
And peyned hire to countrefete cheere
Of court, and to been estatlich of manere,
And to ben holden digne of reverence.
But for to speken of hire conscience,
She was so charitable and so pitous
She wolde wepe, if that she saugh a mous

Kaught in a trappe, if it were deed or bledde.
Of smale houndes hadde she that she fedde
With rosted flessh, or milk and wastel-breed.
But soore wepte she if oon of hem were deed,
Or if men smoot it with a yerde smerte;
And al was conscience and tendre herte.
Ful semyly hir wympul pynched was,
Hir nose *tretys*, hir eyen greye as glas,
Hir mouth ful smal, and therto softe and reed.
But sikerly she hadde a fair forheed;
It was almoost a spanne brood, I trowe;
For, hardily, she was nat undergrowe.
Ful fetys was hir cloke, as I was war.
Of smal coral aboute hire arm she bar
A peire of bedes, gauded al with grene,
And theron heng a brooch of gold ful sheene,
On which ther was first write a crowned A,
And after *Amor vincit omnia*.

But nathelees, whil I have tyme and space,
Er that I ferther in this tale pace,
Me thynketh it acordaunt to resoun
To telle yow al the condicioun
Of ech of hem, so as it semed me,
And whiche they weren, and of what degree,
And eek in what array that they were inne;
And at a knyght than wol I first bigynne.

A Knyght ther was, and that a worthy man,
That fro the tyme that he first bigan
To riden out, he loved chivalrie,

Trouthe and honour, fredom and curteisie.
Ful worthy was he in his lordes werre,
And therto hadde he riden, no man ferre,
As wel in cristendom as in hethenesse,
And evere honoured for his worthynesse;
At Alisaundre he was whan it was wonne.
Ful ofte tyme he hadde the bord bigonne
Aboven alle nacions in Pruce;
In Lettow hadde he reysed and in Ruce,
No Cristen man so ofte of his degree.
In Gernade at the seege eek hadde he be
Of Algezir, and riden in Belmarye.
At Lyeys was he and at Satalye,
Whan they were wonne, and in the Grete See
At many a noble armee hadde he be.
At mortal batailles hadde he been fiftene,
And foughten for oure feith at Tramyssene
In lystes thries, and ay slayn his foo.
This ilke worthy knyght hadde been also
Somtyme with the lord of Palatye
Agayn another hethen in Turkye;
And everemoore he hadde a sovereyn prys.
And though that he were worthy, he was wys,
And of his port as meeke as is a mayde.
He nevere yet no vileynye ne sayde
In al his lyf unto no maner wight.
He was a verray, parfit gentil knyght.
But for to tellen yow of his array,
His hors were goode, but he was nat gay.

Of fustian he wered a gypon
Al bismotered with his habergeon,
For he was late ycome from his viage,
And wente for to doon his pilgrymage.
   With hym ther was his sone, a yong Squier,
A lovyere and a lusty bacheler,
With lokkes crulle as they were leyd in presse.
Of twenty yeer of age he was, I gesse.
Of his stature he was of evene lengthe,
And wonderly delyvere, and of greet strengthe.
And he hadde been somtyme in chyvachie
In Flaundres, in Artoys, and Pycardie,
And born hym weel, as of so litel space,
In hope to stonden in his lady grace.
Embrouded was he, as it were a meede
Al ful of fresshe floures, whyte and reede.
Syngynge he was, or floytynge, al the day;
He was as fressh as is the month of May.
Short was his gowne, with sleves longe and wyde.
Wel koude he sitte on hors and faire ryde.
He koude songes make and wel endite,
Juste and eek daunce, and weel purtreye and write.
So hoote he lovede that by nyghtertale
He sleep namoore than dooth a nyghtyngale.
Curteis he was, lowely, and servysable,
And carf biforn his fader at the table.

THE MONK

A Monk ther was, a fair for the maistrie,
An outridere, that lovede venerie,
A manly man, to been an abbot able.
Ful many a deyntee hors hadde he in stable,
And whan he rood, men myghte his brydel heere
Gynglen in a whistlynge wynd als cleere
And eek as loude as dooth the chapel belle
Ther as this lord was kepere of the celle.
The reule of Seint Maure or of Seint Beneit –
By cause that it was old and somdel streit
This ilke Monk leet olde thynges pace,
And heeld after the newe world the space.
He yaf nat of that text a pulled hen,
That seith that hunters ben nat hooly men,
Ne that a monk, whan he is recchelees,
Is likned til a fissh that is waterlees –
This is to seyn, a monk out of his cloystre.
But thilke text heeld he nat worth an oystre;
And I seyde his opinion was good.
What sholde he studie and make hymselven wood,
Upon a book in cloystre alwey to poure,
Or swynken with his handes, and laboure,
As Austyn bit? How shal the world be served?
Lat Austyn have his swynk to hym reserved!
Therfore he was a prikasour aright:
Grehoundes he hadde as swift as fowel in flight;

13

Of prikyng and of huntyng for the hare
Was al his lust, for no cost wolde he spare.
I seigh his sleves purfiled at the hond
With grys, and that the fyneste of a lond;
And for to festne his hood under his chyn,
He hadde of gold ywroght a ful curious pyn;
A love-knotte in the gretter ende ther was.
His heed was balled, that shoon as any glas,
And eek his face, as he hadde been enoynt.
He was a lord ful fat and in good poynt;
His eyen stepe, and rollynge in his heed,
That stemed as a forneys of a leed;
His bootes souple, his hors in greet estaat.
Now certeinly he was a fair prelaat;
He was nat pale as a forpyned goost.
A fat swan loved he best of any roost.
His palfrey was as broun as is a berye.

THE FRIAR

A Frere ther was, a wantowne and a merye,
A lymytour, a ful solempne man.
In alle the ordres foure is noon that kan
So muchel of daliaunce and fair langage.
He hadde maad ful many a mariage
Of yonge wommen at his owene cost.
Unto his ordre he was a noble post.
Ful wel biloved and famulier was he
With frankeleyns over al in his contree,
And eek with worthy wommen of the toun;
For he hadde power of confessioun,
As seyde hymself, moore than a curat,
For of his ordre he was licenciat.
Ful swetely herde he confessioun,
And plesaunt was his absolucioun:
He was an esy man to yeve penaunce,
Ther as he wiste to have a good pitaunce.
For unto a povre ordre for to yive
Is signe that a man is wel yshryve;
For if he yaf, he dorste make avaunt,
He wiste that a man was repentaunt;
For many a man so hard is of his herte,
He may nat wepe, althogh hym soore smerte.
Therfore in stede of wepynge and preyeres
Men moote yeve silver to the povre freres.
His typet was ay farsed ful of knyves
And pynnes, for to yeven faire wyves.

And certeinly he hadde a murye note:
Wel koude he synge and pleyen on a rote;
Of yeddynges he baar outrely the pris.
His nekke whit was as the flour-de-lys;
Therto he strong was as a champioun.
He knew the tavernes wel in every toun
And everich hostiler and tappestere
Bet than a lazar or a beggestere,
For unto swich a worthy man as he
Acorded nat, as by his facultee,
To have with sike lazars aqueyntaunce.
It is nat honest; it may nat avaunce,
For to deelen with no swich poraille,
But al with riche and selleres of vitaille.
And over al, ther as profit sholde arise,
Curteis he was and lowely of servyse;
Ther nas no man nowher so vertuous.
He was the beste beggere in his hous;
For thogh a wydwe hadde noght a sho,
So plesaunt was his 'In principio,'
Yet wolde he have a ferthyng, er he wente.
His purchas was wel bettre than his rente.
And rage he koude, as it were right a whelp.
In love-dayes ther koude he muchel help,
For ther he was nat lyk a cloysterer
With a thredbare cope, as is a povre scoler,
But he was lyk a maister or a pope.
Of double worstede was his semycope,

That rounded as a belle out of the presse.
Somwhat he lipsed, for his wantownesse,
To make his Englissh sweete upon his tonge;
And in his harpyng, whan that he hadde songe,
His eyen twynkled in his heed aryght
As doon the sterres in the frosty nyght.
This worthy lymytour was cleped Huberd.

THE WIFE OF BATH

A good Wif was ther of biside Bathe,
But she was somdel deef, and that was scathe.
Of clooth-makyng she hadde swich an haunt
She passed hem of Ypres and of Gaunt.
In al the parisshe wif ne was ther noon
That to the offrynge bifore hire sholde goon;
And if ther dide, certeyn so wrooth was she
That she was out of alle charitee.
Hir coverchiefs ful fyne weren of ground;
I dorste swere they weyeden ten pound
That on a Sonday weren upon hir heed.
Hir hosen weren of fyn scarlet reed,
Ful streite yteyd, and shoes ful moyste and newe.
Boold was hir face, and fair, and reed of hewe.
She was a worthy womman al hir lyve:
Housbondes at chirche dore she hadde fyve,
Withouten oother compaignye in youthe –
But thereof nedeth nat to speke as nowthe.
And thries hadde she been at Jerusalem;
She hadde passed many a straunge strem;
At Rome she hadde been, and at Boloigne,
In Galice at Seint-Jame, and at Coloigne.
She koude muchel of wandrynge by the weye.
Gat-tothed was she, soothly for to seye.
Upon an amblere esily she sat,
Ywympled wel, and on hir heed an hat

As brood as is a bokeler or a targe;
A foot-mantel aboute hir hipes large,
And on hir feet a paire of spores sharpe.
In felaweshipe wel koude she laughe and carpe.
Of remedies of love she knew per chaunce,
For she koude of that art the olde daunce.

THE REEVE'S TALE

At Trumpyngtoun, nat fer fro Cantebrigge,
Ther gooth a brook, and over that a brigge,
Upon the whiche brook ther stant a melle;
And this is verray sooth that I yow telle:
A millere was ther dwellynge many a day.
As any pecok he was proud and gay.
Pipen he koude and fisshe, and nettes beete,
And turne coppes, and wel wrastle and sheete;
Ay by his belt he baar a long panade,
And of a swerd ful trenchant was the blade.
A joly poppere baar he in his pouche;
Ther was no man, for peril, dorste hym touche.
A Sheffeld thwitel baar he in his hose.
Round was his face, and *camus* was his nose;
As piled as an ape was his skulle.
He was a market-betere atte fulle.
Ther dorste no wight hand upon hym legge,
That he ne swoor he sholde anon abegge.
A theef he was for sothe of corn and mele,
And that a sly, and usaunt for to stele.
His name was hoote deynous Symkyn.
A wyf he hadde, ycomen of noble kyn;
The person of the toun hir fader was.
With hire he yaf ful many a panne of bras,
For that Symkyn sholde in his blood allye.
She was yfostred in a nonnerye;

20

For Symkyn wolde no wyf, as he sayde,
But she were wel ynorissed and a mayde,
To saven his estaat of yomanrye.
And she was proud, and peert as is a pye.
A ful fair sighte was it upon hem two;
On halydayes biforn hire wolde he go
With his typet wounde aboute his heed,
And she cam after in a gyte of reed;
And Symkyn hadde hosen of the same.
Ther dorste no wight clepen hire but 'dame';
Was noon so hardy that wente by the weye
That with hire dorste rage or ones pleye,
But if he wolde be slayn of Symkyn
With panade, or with knyf, or boidekyn.
For jalous folk ben perilous everemo –
Algate they wolde hire wyves wenden so.
And eek, for she was somdel smoterlich,
She was as digne as water in a dich,
And ful of hoker and of bisemare.
Hir thoughte that a lady sholde hire spare,
What for hire kynrede and hir nortelrie
That she hadde lerned in the nonnerie.

    A doghter hadde they bitwixe hem two
Of twenty yeer, withouten any mo,
Savynge a child that was of half yeer age;
In cradel it lay and was a propre page.
This wenche thikke and wel ygrowen was,
With kamus nose and eyen greye as glas,

With buttokes brode and brestes rounde and hye.
But right fair was hire heer; I wol nat lye.

   This person of the toun, for she was feir,
In purpos was to maken hire his heir,
Bothe of his catel and his mesuage,
And straunge he made it of hir mariage.
His purpos was for to bistowe hire hye
Into som worthy blood of auncetrye;
For hooly chirches good moot been despended
On hooly chirches blood, that is descended.
Therfore he wolde his hooly blood honoure,
Though that he hooly chirche sholde devoure.

   Greet sokene hath this millere, out of doute,
With whete and malt of al the land aboute;
And nameliche ther was a greet collegge
Men clepen the Soler Halle at Cantebregge;
Ther was hir whete and eek hir malt ygrounde.
And on a day it happed, in a stounde,
Sik lay the maunciple on a maladye;
Men wenden wisly that he sholde dye.
For which this millere stal bothe mele and corn
An hundred tyme moore than biforn;
For therbiforn he stal but curteisly,
But now he was a theef outrageously,
For which the wardeyn chidde and made fare.
But therof sette the millere nat a tare;
He craketh boost, and swoor it was nat so.

   Thanne were ther yonge povre scolers two,

That dwelten in this halle, of which I seye.
Testif they were, and lusty for to pleye,
And, oonly for hire myrthe and revelrye,
Upon the wardeyn bisily they crye
To yeve hem leve, but a litel stounde,
To goon to mille and seen hir corn ygrounde;
And hardily they dorste leye hir nekke
The millere sholde not stele hem half a pekke
Of corn by sleighte, ne by force hem reve;
And at the laste the wardeyn yaf hem leve.
John highte that oon, and Aleyn highte that oother;
Of o toun were they born, that highte Strother,
Fer in the north; I kan nat telle where.

    This Aleyn maketh redy al his gere,
And on an hors the sak he caste anon.
Forth goth Aleyn the clerk, and also John,
With good swerd and with bokeler by hir syde.
John knew the wey – hem nedede no gyde –
And at the mille the sak adoun he layth.
Aleyn spak first: 'Al hayl, Symond, y-fayth!
Hou fares thy faire doghter and thy wyf?'

    'Aleyn, welcome,' quod Symkyn, 'by my lyf!
And John also, how now, what do ye heer?'

    'Symond,' quod John, 'by God, nede has na peer.
Hym boes serve hymself that has na swayn,
Or elles he is a fool, as clerkes sayn.
Oure manciple, I hope he wil be deed,
Swa werkes ay the wanges in his heed;

And forthy is I come, and eek Alayn,
To grynde oure corn and carie it ham agayn;
I pray yow spede us heythen that ye may.'

'It shal be doon,' quod Symkyn, 'by my fay!
What wol ye doon whil that it is in hande?'

'By God, right by the hopur wil I stande,'
Quod John, 'and se howgates the corn gas in.
Yet saugh I nevere, by my fader kyn,
How that the hopur wagges til and fra.'

Aleyn answerde, 'John, and wiltow swa?
Thanne wil I be bynethe, by my croun,
And se how that the mele falles doun
Into the trough; that sal be my disport.
For John, y-faith, I may been of youre sort;
I is as ille a millere as ar ye.'

This millere smyled of hir nycetee,
And thoughte, 'Al this nys doon but for a wyle.
They wene that no man may hem bigyle,
But by my thrift, yet shal I blere hir ye,
For al the sleighte in hir philosophye.
The moore queynte crekes that they make,
The moore wol I stele whan I take.
In stide of flour yet wol I yeve hem bren.
"The gretteste clerkes been noght wisest men,"
As whilom to the wolf thus spak the mare.
Of al hir art counte I noght a tare.'

Out at the dore he gooth ful pryvely,
Whan that he saugh his tyme, softely.

24

He looketh up and doun til he hath founde
The clerkes hors, ther as it stood ybounde
Bihynde the mille, under a levesel;
And to the hors he goth hym faire and wel;
He strepeth of the brydel right anon.
And whan the hors was laus, he gynneth gon
Toward the fen, ther wilde mares renne,
And forth with 'wehee,' thurgh thikke and thurgh
    thenne.

    This millere gooth agayn, no word he seyde,
But dooth his note, and with the clerkes pleyde
Til that hir corn was faire and weel ygrounde.
And whan the mele is sakked and ybounde,
This John goth out and fynt his hors away,
And gan to crie 'Harrow!' and 'Weylaway!
Oure hors is lorn, Alayn, for Goddes banes,
Step on thy feet! Com of, man, al atanes!
Allas, our wardeyn has his palfrey lorn,'
This Aleyn al forgat, bothe mele and corn;
Al was out of his mynde his housbondrie.
'What, whilk way is he geen?' he gan to crie.

    The wyf cam lepynge inward with a ren.
She seyde, 'Allas! youre hors goth to the fen
With wilde mares, as faste as he may go.
Unthank come on his hand that boond hym so,
And he that bettre sholde han knyt the reyne!'

    'Allas,' quod John, 'Aleyn, for Cristes peyne
Lay doun thy swerd, and I wil myn alswa.
I is ful wight, God waat, as is a raa;

25

By Goddes herte, he sal nat scape us bathe!
Why ne had thow pit the capul in the lathe?
Ilhayl! By God, Alayn, thou is a fonne!'

    Thise sely clerkes han ful faste yronne
Toward the fen, bothe Aleyn and eek John.

    And whan the millere saugh that they were gon,
He half a busshel of hir flour hath take,
And bad his wyf go knede it in a cake.
He seyde, 'I trowe the clerkes were aferd.
Yet kan a millere make a clerkes berd,
For al his art; now lat hem goon hir weye!
Lo, wher he gooth! Ye, lat the children pleye.
They gete hym nat so lightly, by my croun.'

    Thise sely clerkes rennen up and doun
With 'Keep! Keep! Stand! Stand! Jossa, warderere,
Ga whistle thou, and I shal kepe hym heere!'
But shortly, til that it was verray nyght,
They koude nat, though they dide al hir myght,
Hir capul cacche, he ran alwey so faste,
Til in a dych they caughte hym atte laste.

    Wery and weet, as beest is in the reyn,
Comth sely John, and with him comth Aleyn.
'Allas,' quod John, 'the day that I was born!
Now are we dryve til hethyng and til scorn.
Oure corn is stoln; men wil us fooles calle,
Bathe the wardeyn and oure felawes alle,
And namely the millere, weylaway!'

    Thus pleyneth John as he gooth by the way

Toward the mille, and Bayard in his hond.
The millere sittynge by the fyr he fond,
For it was nyght, and forther myghte they noght;
But for the love of God they hym bisoght
Of herberwe and of ese, as for hir peny.

   The millere seyde agayn, 'If ther be eny,
Swich as it is, yet shal ye have youre part.
Myn hous is streit, but ye han lerned art;
Ye konne by argumentes make a place
A myle brood of twenty foot of space.
Lat se now if this place may suffise,
Or make it rowm with speche, as is youre gise.'

   'Now, Symond,' seyde John, 'by Seint Cutberd,
Ay is thou myrie, and this is faire answerd.
I have herd seyd, "Man sal taa of twa thynges:
Slyk as he fyndes, or taa slyk as he brynges."
But specially I pray thee, hooste deere,
Get us som mete and drynke, and make us cheere,
And we wil payen trewely atte fulle.
With empty hand men may na haukes tulle;
Loo, heere oure silver, redy for to spende.'

   This millere into toun his doghter sende
For ale and breed, and rosted hem a goos,
And boond hire hors, it sholde namoore go loos,
And in his owene chambre hem made a bed,
With sheetes and with chalons faire yspred
Noght from his owene bed ten foot or twelve.
His doghter hadde a bed, al by hirselve,

Right in the same chambre by and by.
It myghte be no bet, and cause why?
Ther was no roumer herberwe in the place.
They soupen and they speke, hem to solace,
And drynken evere strong ale atte beste.
Aboute mydnyght wente they to reste.

Wel hath this millere vernysshed his heed;
Ful pale he was for dronken, and nat reed.
He yexeth, and he speketh thurgh the nose
As he were on the quakke, or on the pose.
To bedde he goth, and with hym goth his wyf.
As any jay she light was and jolyf,
So was hir joly whistle wel ywet.
The cradel at hir beddes feet is set,
To rokken, and to yeve the child to sowke.
And whan that dronken al was in the crowke,
To bedde wente the doghter right anon;
To bedde goth Aleyn and also John;
Ther nas na moore – hem nedede no dwale.
This millere hath so wisely bibbed ale
That as an hors he fnorteth in his sleep,
Ne of his tayl bihynde he took no keep.
His wyf bar hym a burdon, a ful strong;
Men myghte hir rowtyng heere two furlong;
The wenche rowteth eek, par compaignye.

Aleyn the clerk, that herde this melodye,
He poked John, and seyde, 'Slepestow?
Herdestow evere slyk a sang er now?

Lo, swilk a complyn is ymel hem alle;
A wilde fyr upon thair bodyes falle!
Wha herkned evere slyk a ferly thyng?
Ye, they sal have the flour of il endyng.
This lange nyght ther tydes me na reste;
But yet, na fors, al sal be for the beste.
For, John,' seyde he, 'als evere moot I thryve,
If that I may, yon wenche wil I swyve.
Som esement has lawe yshapen us,
For, John, ther is a lawe that says thus:
That gif a man in a point be agreved,
That in another he sal be releved.
Oure corn is stoln, sothly, it is na nay,
And we han had an il fit al this day;
And syn I sal have neen amendement
Agayn my los, I will have esement.
By Goddes sale, it sal neen other bee!'

    This John answerde, 'Alayn, avyse thee!
The millere is a perilous man,' he seyde,
'And gif that he out of his sleep abreyde,
He myghte doon us bethe a vileynye.'

    Aleyn answerde, 'I counte hym nat a flye.'
And up he rist, and by the wenche he crepte.
This wenche lay uprighte and faste slepte,
Til he so ny was, er she myghte espie,
That it had been to late for to crie,
And shortly for to seyn, they were aton.
Now pley, Aleyn, for I wol speke of John.

This John lith stille a furlong wey or two,
And to hymself he maketh routhe and wo.
'Allas!' quod he, 'this is a wikked jape;
Now may I seyn that I is but an *ape*.
Yet has my felawe somwhat for his harm;
He has the milleris doghter in his arm.
He auntred hym, and has his nedes sped,
And I lye as a draf-sak in my bed;
And when this jape is tald another day,
I sal been halde a daf, a cokenay!
I wil arise and auntre it, by my fayth!
"Unhardy is unseely," thus men sayth.'
And up he roos, and softely he wente
Unto the cradel, and in his hand it hente,
And baar it softe unto his beddes feet.

Soone after this the wyf hir rowtyng leet,
And gan awake, and wente hire out to pisse,
And cam agayn, and gan hir cradel mysse,
And groped heer and ther, but she foond noon.
'Allas!' quod she, 'I hadde almoost mysgoon;
I hadde almoost goon to the clerkes bed.
Ey, benedicite! Thanne hadde I foule ysped!'
And forth she gooth til she the cradel fond.
She gropeth alwey forther with hir hond,
And foond the bed, and thoghte noght but good,
By cause that the cradel by it stood,
And nyste wher she was, for it was derk;
But faire and wel she creep in to the clerk,

And lith ful stille, and wolde han caught a sleep.
Withinne a while this John the clerk up leep,
And on this goode wyf he leith on soore.
So myrie a fit ne hadde she nat ful yoore;
He priketh harde and depe as he were mad.
This joly lyf han thise two clerkes lad
Til that the thridde cok bigan to synge.

    Aleyn wax wery in the dawenynge,
For he had swonken al the longe nyght,
And seyde, 'Fare weel, Malyne, sweete wight!
The day is come; I may no lenger byde;
But everemo, wher so I go or ryde,
I is thyn awen clerk, swa have I seel!'
'Now, deere lemman,' quod she, 'go, far weel!
But er thow go, o thyng I wol thee telle:
Whan that thou wendest homward by the melle,
Right at the entree of the dore bihynde
Thou shalt a cake of half a busshel fynde
That was ymaked of thyn owene mele,
Which that I heelp my sire for to stele.
And, goode lemman, God thee save and kepe!'
And with that word almoost she gan to wepe.

    Aleyn up rist, and thoughte, 'Er that it dawe,
I wol go crepen in by my felawe,'
And fond the cradel with his hand anon.
'By God,' thoughte he, 'al wrang I have mysgon.
Myn heed is toty of my swynk to-nyght,
That makes me that I ga nat aright.

I woot wel by the cradel I have mysgo;
Heere lith the millere and his wyf also.'
And forth he goth, a twenty devel way,
Unto the bed ther as the millere lay.
He wende have cropen by his felawe John,
And by the millere in he creep anon,
And caughte hym by the nekke, and softe he spak.
He seyde, 'Thou John, thou swynes-heed, awak,
For Cristes saule, and heer a noble game.
For by that lord that called is Seint Jame,
As I have thries in this shorte nyght
Swyved the milleres doghter bolt upright,
Whil thow hast, as a coward, been agast.'

   'Ye, false harlot,' quod the millere, 'hast?
A, false traitour! False clerk!' quod he,
Thow shalt be deed, by Goddes dignitee!
Who dorste be so boold to disparage
My doghter, that is come of swich lynage?'
And by the throte-bolle he caughte Alayn,
And he hente hym despitously agayn,
And on the nose he smoot hym with his fest.
Doun ran the blody streem upon his brest;
And in the floor, with nose and mouth tobroke,
They walwe as doon two pigges in a poke;
And up they goon, and doun agayn anon,
Til that the millere sporned at a stoon,
And doun he fil bakward upon his wyf,
That wiste no thyng of this nyce stryf;

For she was falle aslepe a lite wight
With John the clerk, that waked hadde al nyght,
And with the fal out of hir sleep she breyde.
'Help! hooly croys of Bromeholm,' she seyde,
'In manus tuas! Lord, to thee I calle!
Awak, Symond! The feend is on me falle.
Myn herte is broken; help! I nam but deed!
Ther lyth oon upon my wombe and on myn heed.
Help, Symkyn, for the false clerkes fighte!'
  This John stirte up as faste as ever he myghte,
And graspeth by the walles to and fro,
To fynde a staf; and she stirte up also,
And knew the estres bet than dide this John,
And by the wal a staf she foond anon,
And saugh a litel shymeryng of a light,
For at an hole in shoon the moone bright,
And by that light she saugh hem bothe two,
But sikerly she nyste who was who,
But as she saugh a whit thyng in hir ye.
And whan she gan this white thyng espye,
She wende the clerk hadde wered a volupeer,
And with the staf she drow ay neer and neer,
And wende han hit this Aleyn at the fulle,
And smoot the millere on the pyled skulle,
That doun he gooth, and cride, 'Harrow! I dye!'
Thise clerkes beete hym weel and lete hym lye,
And greythen hem, and tooke hir hors anon,
And eek hire mele, and on hir wey they gon.

33

And at the mille yet they tooke hir cake
Of half a busshel flour, ful wel ybake.
    Thus is the proude millere wel ybete,
And hath ylost the gryndynge of the whete,
And payed for the soper everideel
Of Aleyn and of John, that bette hym weel.
His wyf is swyved, and his doghter als.
Lo, swich it is a millere to be fals!
And therfore this proverbe is seyd ful sooth,
'Hym thar nat wene wel that yvele dooth.'
A gylour shal hymself bigyled be.
And God, that sitteth heighe in magestee,
Save al this compaignye, grete and smale!
Thus have I quyt the Millere in my tale.

THE FRANKLIN'S TALE

In Armorik, that called is Britayne,
Ther was a knyght that loved and dide his payne
To serve a lady in his beste wise;
And many a labour, many a greet emprise,
He for his lady wroghte er she were wonne.
For she was oon the faireste under sonne,
And eek therto comen of so heigh kynrede
That wel unnethes dorste this knyght, for drede,
Telle hire his wo, his peyne, and his distresse.
But atte laste she, for his worthynesse,
And namely for his meke obeysaunce,
Hath swich a pitee caught of his penaunce
That pryvely she fil of his accord
To take hym for hir housbonde and hir lord,
Of swich lordshipe as men han over hir wyves.
And for to lede the moore in blisse hir lyves,
Of his free wyl he swoor hire as a knyght
That nevere in al his lyf he, day ne nyght,
Ne sholde upon hym take no maistrie
Agayn hir wyl, ne kithe hire jalousie,
But hire obeye, and folwe hir wyl in al,
As any lovere to his lady shal,
Save that the name of soveraynetee,
That wolde he have for shame of his degree.
  She thanked hym, and with ful greet humblesse
She seyde, 'Sire, sith of youre gentillesse
Ye profre me to have so large a reyne,

Ne wolde nevere God bitwixe us tweyne,
As in my gilt, were outher werre or stryf.
Sire, I wol be youre humble trewe wyf –
Have heer my trouthe – til that myn herte breste.'
Thus been they bothe in quiete and in reste.

   For o thyng, sires, saufly dar I seye,
That freendes everych oother moot obeye,
If they wol longe holden compaignye.
Love wol nat been constreyned by maistrye.
Whan maistrie comth, the God of Love anon
Beteth his wynges, and farewel, he is gon!
Love is a thyng as any spirit free.
Wommen, of kynde, desiren libertee,
And nat to been constreyned as a thral;
And so doon men, if I sooth seyen shal.
Looke who that is moost pacient in love,
He is at his avantage al above.
Pacience is an heigh vertu, certeyn,
For it venquysseth, as thise clerkes seyn,
Thynges that rigour sholde nevere atteyne.
For every word men may nat chide or pleyne.
Lerneth to suffre, or elles, so moot I goon,
Ye shul it lerne, wher so ye wole or noon;
For in this world, certein, ther no wight is
That he ne dooth or seith somtyme amys.
Ire, siknesse, or constellacioun,
Wyn, wo, or chaungynge of complexioun
Causeth ful ofte to doon amys or speken.
On every wrong a man may nat be wreken.

After the tyme moste be temperaunce
To every wight that kan on governaunce.
And therfore hath this wise, worthy knyght,
To lyve in ese, suffrance hire bihight,
And she to hym ful wisly gan to swere
That nevere sholde ther be defaute in here.

    Heere may men seen an humble, wys accord;
Thus hath she take hir servant and hir lord –
Servant in love, and lord in mariage.
Thanne was he bothe in lordshipe and servage.
Servage? Nay, but in lordshipe above,
Sith he hath bothe his lady and his love;
His lady, certes, and his wyf also,
The which that lawe of love acordeth to.
And whan he was in this prosperitee,
Hoom with his wyf he gooth to his contree,
Nat fer fro Pedmark, ther his dwellyng was,
Where as he lyveth in blisse and in solas.

    Who koude telle, but he hadde wedded be,
The joye, the ese, and the prosperitee
That is bitwixe an housbonde and his wyf?
A yeer and moore lasted this blisful lyf,
Til that the knyght of which I speke of thus,
That of Kayrrud was cleped Arveragus,
Shoop hym to goon and dwelle a yeer or tweyne
In Engelond, that cleped was eek Briteyne,
To seke in armes worshipe and honour –
For al his lust he sette in swich labour –
And dwelled there two yeer; the book seith thus.

Now wol I stynten of this Arveragus,
And speken I wole of Dorigen his wyf,
That loveth hire housbonde as hire hertes lyf.
For his absence wepeth she and siketh,
As doon thise noble wyves whan hem liketh.
She moorneth, waketh, wayleth, fasteth, pleyneth;
Desir of his presence hire so destreyneth
That al this wyde world she sette at noght.
Hire freendes, whiche that knewe hir hevy thoght,
Conforten hire in al that ever they may.
They prechen hire, they telle hire nyght and day
That causelees she sleeth hirself, allas!
And every confort possible in this cas
They doon to hire with al hire bisynesse,
Al for to make hire leve hire hevynesse.

By proces, as ye knowen everichoon,
Men may so longe graven in a stoon
Til som figure therinne emprented be.
So longe han they conforted hire til she
Receyved hath, by hope and by resoun,
The emprentyng of hire consolacioun,
Thurgh which hir grete sorwe gan aswage;
She may nat alwey duren in swich rage.

And eek Arveragus, in al this care,
Hath sent hire lettres hoom of his welfare,
And that he wol come hastily agayn;
Or elles hadde this sorwe hir herte slayn.

Hire freendes sawe hir sorwe gan to slake
And preyde hire on knees, for Goddes sake,

To come and romen hire in compaignye,
Awey to dryve hire derke fantasye.
And finally she graunted that requeste,
For wel she saugh that it was for the beste.

  Now stood hire castel faste by the see,
And often with hire freendes walketh shee
Hire to disporte upon the bank an heigh,
Where as she many a ship and barge seigh
Seillynge hir cours, where as hem liste go.
But thanne was that a parcel of hire wo,
For to hirself ful ofte, 'Allas!' seith she,
'Is ther no ship, of so manye as I se,
Wol bryngen hom my lord? Thanne were myn herte
Al warisshed of his bittre peynes smerte.'

  Another tyme ther wolde she sitte and thynke,
And caste hir eyen dounward for the brynke.
But whan she saugh the grisly rokkes blake,
For verray feere so wolde hir herte quake
That on hire feet she myghte hire noght sustene.
Thanne wolde she sitte adoun upon the grene,
And pitously into the see biholde,
And seyn right thus, with sorweful sikes colde:

  'Eterne God, that thurgh thy purveiaunce
Ledest the world by certein governaunce,
In ydel, as men seyn, ye no thyng make.
But, Lord, thise grisly feeendly rokkes blake,
That semen rather a foul confusion
Of werk than any fair creacion
Of swich a parfit wys God and a stable,

Why han ye wroght this werk unresonable?
For by this werk, south, north, ne west, ne eest,
Ther nys yfostred man, ne bryd, ne beest;
It dooth no good, to my wit, but anoyeth.
Se ye nat, Lord, how mankynde it destroyeth?
An hundred thousand bodyes of mankynde
Han rokkes slayn, al be they nat in mynde,
Which mankynde is so fair part of thy werk
That thou it madest lyk to thyn owene merk.
Thanne semed it ye hadde a greet chiertee
Toward mankynde; but how thanne may it bee
That ye swiche meenes make it to destroyen,
Whiche meenes do no good, but evere anoyen?
I woot wel clerkes wol seyn as hem leste,
By argumentz, that al is for the beste,
Though I ne kan the causes nat yknowe.
But thilke God that made wynd to blowe
As kepe my lord! This my conclusion.
To clerkes lete I al disputison.
But wolde God that alle thise rokkes blake
Were sonken into helle for his sake!
Thise rokkes sleen myn herte for the feere.'
Thus wolde she seyn, with many a pitous teere.

　　Hire freendes sawe that it was no disport
To romen by the see, but disconfort,
And shopen for to pleyen somwher elles.
They leden hire by ryveres and by welles,
And eek in othere places delitables;
They dauncen and they pleyen at ches and tables.

So on a day, right in the morwe-tyde,
Unto a gardyn that was there bisyde,
In which that they hadde maad hir ordinaunce
Of vitaille and of oother purveiaunce,
They goon and pleye hem al the longe day.
And this was on the sixte morwe of May,
Which May hadde peynted with his softe shoures
This gardyn ful of leves and of floures;
And craft of mannes hand so curiously
Arrayed hadde this gardyn, trewely,
That nevere was ther gardyn of swich prys
But if it were the verray paradys.
The odour of floures and the fresshe sighte
Wolde han maked any herte lighte
That evere was born, but if to greet siknesse
Or to greet sorwe helde it in distresse,
So ful it was of beautee with plesaunce.
At after-dyner gonne they to daunce,
And synge also, save Dorigen allone,
Which made alwey hir compleint and hir moone,
For she ne saugh hym on the daunce go
That was hir housbonde and hir love also.
But nathelees she moste a tyme abyde
And with good hope lete hir sorwe slyde.

Upon this daunce, amonges othere men,
Daunced a squier biforn Dorigen,
That fressher was and jolyer of array,
As to my doom, than is the month of May.
He syngeth, daunceth, passynge any man

That is, or was, sith that the world bigan.
Therwith he was, if men sholde hymn discryve,
Oon of the beste farynge man on lyve;
Yong, strong, right vertuous, and riche, and wys,
And wel biloved, and holden in greet prys.
And shortly, if the sothe I tellen shal,
Unwityng of this Dorigen at al,
This lusty squier, servant to Venus,
Which that ycleped was Aurelius,
Hadde loved hire best of any creature
Two yeer and moore, as was his aventure,
But nevere dorste he tellen hire his grevaunce.
Withouten coppe he drank al his penaunce.
He was despeyred; no thyng dorste he seye,
Save in his songes somwhat wolde he wreye
His wo, as in a general compleynyng;
He seyde he lovede and was biloved no thyng.
Of swich matere made he manye layes,
Songes, compleintes, roundels, virelayes,
How that he dorste nat his sorwe telle,
But langwissheth as a furye dooth in helle;
And dye he moste, he seyde, as dide Ekko
For Narcisus, that dorste nat telle hir wo.
In oother manere than ye heere me seye,
Ne dorste he nat to hire his wo biwreye,
Save that, paraventure, somtyme at daunces,
Ther yonge folk kepen hir observaunces,
It may wel be he looked on hir face
In swich a wise as man that asketh grace;

But nothyng wiste she of his entente.
Natheless it happed, er they thennes wente,
By cause that he was hire neighebour,
And was a man of worshipe and honour,
And hadde yknowen hym of tyme yoore,
They fille in speche; and forth, moore and moore,
Unto his purpos drough Aurelius,
And whan he saugh his tyme, he seyde thus:
    'Madame,' quod he, 'by God that this world made,
So that I wiste it myghte youre herte glade,
I wolde that day that youre Arveragus
Wente over the see, that I, Aurelius,
Hadde went ther nevere I sholde have come agayn.
For wel I woot my servyce is in vayn;
My gerdon is but brestyng of myn herte.
Madame, reweth upon my peynes smerte;
For with a word ye may me sleen or save.
Heere at youre feet God wolde that I were grave!
I ne have as now no leyser moore to seye;
Have mercy, sweete, or ye wol do me deye!'
    She gan to looke upon Aurelius;
'Is this youre wyl,' quod she, 'and sey ye thus?
Nevere erst,' quod she, 'ne wiste I what ye mente.
But now, Aurelie, I knowe youre entente,
By thilke God that yaf me soule and lyf,
Ne shal I nevere been untrewe wyf
In word ne werk, as fer as I have wit;
I wol been his to whom that I am knyt.
Taak this for fynal answere as of me.'

But after that in pley thus seyde she:

'Aurelie,' quod she, 'by heighe God above,
Yet wolde I graunte yow to been youre love,
Syn I yow se so pitously complayne.
Looke what day that endeong Britayne
Ye remoeve alle the rokkes, stoon by stoon,
That they ne lette ship ne boot to goon –
I seye, whan ye han maad the coost so clene
Of rokkes that ther nys no stoon ysene,
Thanne wol I love yow best of any man;
Have heer my trouthe, in al that evere I kan.'

'Is ther noon oother grace in yow?' quod he.

'No, by that Lord,' quod she, 'that maked me!
For wel I woot that it shal never bityde.
Lat swiche folies out of youre herte slyde.
What deyntee sholde a man han in his lyf
For to go love another mannes wyf,
That hath hir body whan so that hym liketh?'

Aurelius ful ofte soore siketh;
Wo was Aurelie whan that he this herde,
And with a sorweful herte he thus answerde:

'Madame,' quod he, 'this were an inpossible!
Thanne moot I dye of sodeyn deth horrible.'
And with that word he turned hym anon.
Tho coome hir othere freendes many oon,
And in the aleyes romeden up and doun,
And nothyng wiste of this conclusioun,
But sodeynly bigonne revel newe
Til that the brighte soone loste his hewe;

44

For th'orisonte hath reft the soone his lyght –
This is as muche to seye as it was nyght –
And hoom they goon in joye and in solas,
Save oonly wrecche Aurelius, allas!
He to his hous is goon with sorweful herte.
He seeth he may nat fro his deeth asterte;
Hym semed that he felte his herte colde.
Up to the hevene his handes he gan holde,
And on his knowes bare he sette hym doun,
And in his ravyng seyde his orisoun.
For verray wo out of his wit he breyde.
He nyste what he spak, but thus he seyde;
With pitous herte his pleynt hath he bigonne
Unto the goddes, and first unto the sonne:

He seyde, 'Appollo, god and governour
Of every plaunte, herbe, tree, and flour,
That yevest, after thy declinacion,
To ech of hem his tyme and his seson,
As thyn herberwe chaungeth lowe or heighe,
Lord Phebus, cast thy merciable eighe
On wrecche Aurelie, which that am but lorn.
Lo, lord! My lady hath my deeth ysworn
Withoute gilt, but thy benignytee
Upon my dedly herte have som pitee.
For wel I woot, lord Phebus, if yow lest,
Ye may me helpen, save my lady, best.
Now voucheth sauf that I may yow devyse
How that I may been holpen and in what wyse.

'Youre blisful suster, Lucina the sheene,

That of the see is chief goddesse and queene
(Though Neptunus have deitee in the see,
Yet emperisse aboven hym is she),
Ye knowen wel, lord, that right as hir desir
Is to be quyked and lighted of youre fir,
For which she folweth yow ful bisily,
Right so the see desireth naturelly
To folwen hire, as she that is goddesse
Bothe in the see and ryveres moore and lesse.
Wherefore, lord Phebus, this is my requeste –
Do this miracle, or do myn herte breste –
That now next at this opposicion
Which in the signe shal be of the Leon,
As preieth hire so greet a flood to brynge
That fyve fadme at the leeste it oversprynge
The hyeste rokke in Armorik Briteyne;
And lat this flood endure yeres tweyne.
Thanne certes to my lady may I seye,
"Holdeth youre heste, the rokkes been aweye."

    'Lord Phebus, dooth this miracle for me.
Preye hire she go no faster cours than ye;
I seye, preyeth your suster that she go
No faster cours than ye thise yeres two.
Thanne shal she been evene atte fulle alway,
And spryng flood laste bothe nyght and day.
And but she vouche sauf in swich manere
To graunte me my sovereyn lady deere,
Prey hire to synken every rok adoun
Into hir owene dirke regioun

46

Under the ground, ther Pluto dwelleth inne,
Or nevere mo shal I my lady wynne.
Thy temple in Delphos wol I barefoot seke.
Lord Phebus, se the teeris on my cheke,
And of my peyne have som compassioun.'
And with that word in swowne he fil adoun,
And longe tyme he lay forth in a traunce.

His brother, which that knew of his penaunce,
Up caughte hym and to bedde he hath hym broght.
Dispeyred in this torment and this thoght
Lete I this woful creature lye;
Chese he, for me, wheither he wol lyve or dye.

Arveragus, with heele and greet honour,
As he that was of chivalrie the flour,
Is comen hoom, and othere worthy men.
O blisful artow now, thou Dorigen,
That hast thy lusty housbonde in thyne armes,
The fresshe knyght, the worthy man of armes,
That loveth thee as his owene hertes lyf.
No thyng list hym to been ymaginatyf,
If any wight hadde spoke, whil he was oute,
To hire of love; he hadde of it no doute.
He noght entendeth to no swich mateere,
But daunceth, justeth, maketh hire good cheere;
And thus in joye and blisse I lete hem dwelle,
And of the sike Aurelis wol I telle.

In langour and in torment furyus
Two yeer and moore lay wrecche Aurelyus,
Er any foot he myghte on erthe gon;

Ne confort in this tyme hadde he noon,
Save of his brother, which that was a clerk.
He knew of al this wo and al this werk,
For to noon oother creature, certeyn,
Of this matere he dorste no word seyn.
Under his brest he baar it moore secree
Than evere dide Pamphilus for Galathee.
His brest was hool, withoute for to sene,
But in his herte ay was the arwe kene.
And wel ye knowe that of a sursanure
In surgerye is perilous the cure,
But men myghte touche the arwe or come therby.
His brother weep and wayled pryvely,
Til atte laste hym fil in remembraunce,
That whiles he was at Orliens in Fraunce –
As yonge clerkes that been lykerous
To reden artes that been curious
Seken in every halke and every herne
Particuler sciences for to lerne –
He hym remembred that, upon a day,
At Orliens in studie a book he say
Of magyk natureel, which his felawe,
That was that tyme a bacheler of lawe,
Al were he ther to lerne another craft,
Hadde prively upon his desk ylaft;
Which book spak muchel of the operaciouns
Touchynge the eighte and twenty mansiouns
That longen to the moone, and swich folye
As in oure dayes is nat worth a flye –

48

For hooly chirches feith in oure bileve
Ne suffreth noon illusioun us to greve.
And whan this book was in his remembraunce,
Anon for joye his herte gan to daunce,
And to hymself he seyde pryvely:
'My brother shal be warisshed hastily;
For I am siker that ther be sciences
By whiche men make diverse apparences,
Swiche as thise subtile tregetoures pleye.
For ofte at feestes have I wel herd seye
That tregetours withinne an halle large
Have maad come in a water and a barge,
And in the halle rowen up and doun.
Somtyme hath semed come a grym leoun;
And somtyme floures sprynge as in a mede;
Somtyme a vyne, and grapes white and rede;
Somtyme a castel, al of lym and stoon;
And whan hem lyked, voyded it anon.
Thus semed it to every mannes sighte.
   'Now thanne conclude I thus: that if I myghte
At Orliens som oold felawe yfynde
That hadde thise moones mansions in mynde,
Or oother magyk natureel above,
He sholde wel make my brother han his love.
For with an apparence a clerk may make,
To mannes sighte, that alle the rokkes blake
Of Britaigne wren yvoyded everichon,
And shippes by the brynke comen and gon,
And in swich forme enduren a wowke or two.

Thanne were my brother warisshed of his wo;
Thanne moste she nedes holden hire biheste,
Or elles he shal shame hire atte leeste.'
  What sholde I make a lenger tale of this?
Unto his brotheres bed he comen is,
And swich confort he yaf hym for to gon
To Orliens that he up stirte anon,
And on his wey forthward thanne is he fare
In hope for to been lissed of his care,
  Whan they were come almoost to that citee,
But if it were a two furlong or thre,
A yong clerk romynge by hymself they mette,
Which that in Latyn thriftily hem grette,
And after that he seyde a wonder thyng:
'I knowe,' quod he, 'the cause of youre comyng.'
And er they ferther any foote wente,
He tolde hem al that was in hire entente.
  This Briton clerk hym asked of felawes
The whiche that he had knowe in olde dawes,
And he answerde hym that they dede were,
For which he weep ful ofte many a teere.
  Doun of his hors Aurelius lighte anon,
And with this magicien forth is he gon
Hoom to his hous, and maden hem wel at ese.
Hem lakked no vitaille that myghte hem plese.
So wel arrayed hous as ther was oon
Aurelius in his lyf saugh nevere noon.
  He shewed hym, er he wente to sopeer,
Forestes, parkes ful of wilde deer;

Ther saugh he hertes with hir hornes hye,
The gretteste that evere were seyn with ye.
He saugh of hem an hondred slayn with houndes,
And somme with arwes blede of bittre woundes.
He saugh, whan voyded were thise wilde deer,
Thise fauconers upon a fair ryver,
That with hir haukes han the heron slayn.

  Tho saugh he knyghtes justyng in a playn;
And after this he dide hym swich plesaunce
That he hym shewed his lady on a daunce,
On which hymself he daunced, as hym thoughte.
And whan this maister that this magyk wroughte
Saugh it was tyme, he clapte his handes two,
And farewel! Al oure revel was ago.
And yet remoeved they nevere out of the hous,
Whil they saugh al this sighte merveillous,
But in his studie, ther as his bookes be,
They seten stille, and no wight but they thre.

  To hym this maister called his squier,
And seyde hym thus: 'Is redy oure soper?
Almoost an houre it is, I undertake,
Sith I yow bad oure soper for to make,
Whan that thise worthy men wenten with me
Into my studie, ther as my bookes be.'

  'Sire,' quod this squier, 'whan it liketh yow,
It is al redy, though ye wol right now.'
'Go we thanne soupe,' quod he, 'as for the beste.
Thise amorous folk somtyme moote han hir reste.'

  At after-soper fille they in tretee

What somme sholde this maistres gerdon be
To remoeven alle the rokkes of Britayne,
And eek from Gerounde to the mouth of Sayne.

He made it straunge, and swoor, so God hym save,
Lasse than a thousand pound he wolde nat have,
Ne gladly for that somme he wolde nat goon.

Aurelius, with blisful herte anoon,
Answerde thus: 'Fy on a thousand pound!
This wyde world, which that men seye is round,
I wolde it yeve, if I were lord of it.
This bargayn is ful dryve, for we been kynt,
Ye shal be payed trewely, by my trouthe!
But looketh now, for no necligence or slouthe
Ye tarie us heere no lenger than to-morwe.'

'Nay,' quod this clerk, 'have heer my feith
   to borwe.'

To bedde is goon Aurelius whan hym leste,
And wel ny al that nyght he hadde his reste.
What for his labour and his hope of blisse,
His woful herte of penaunce hadde a lisse.

Upon the morwe, whan that it was day,
To Britaigne tooke they the righte way,
Aurelius and this magicien bisyde,
And been descended ther they wolde abyde.
And this was, as thise bookes me remembre,
The colde, frosty seson of Decembre.

Phebus wax old, and hewed lyk laton,
That in his hoote declynacion
Shoon as the burned gold with stremes brighte;

But now in Capricorn adoun he lighte,
Where as he shoon ful pale, I dar wel seyn.
The bittre frostes, with the sleet and reyn,
Destroyed hath the grene in every yerd.
Janus sit by the fyr, with double berd,
And drynketh of his bugle horn the wyn;
Biforn hym stant brawen of the tusked swyn,
And 'Nowel' crieth every lusty man.

Aurelius in al that evere he kan
Dooth to this maister chiere and reverence,
And preyeth hym to doon his diligence
To bryngen hym out of his peynes smerte,
Or with a swerd that he wolde slitte his herte.

This subtil clerk swich routhe had of this man
That nyght and day he spedde hym that he kan
To wayten a tyme of his conclusioun;
This is to seye, to maken illusioun,
By swich an apparence or jogelrye –
I ne kan no termes of astrologye –
That she and every wight sholde wene and seye
That of Britaigne the rokkes were aweye,
Or ellis they were sonken under grounde.
So atte laste he hath his tyme yfounde
To maken his japes and his wrecchednesse
Of swich a supersticious cursednesse.
His table Tolletanes forth he brought,
Ful wel corrected, ne ther lakked nought,
Neither his collect ne his expans yeeris,
Ne his rootes, ne his othere geeris,

As been his cenris and his argumentz
And his proporcioneles convenientz
For his equacions in every thyng.
And by his eighte speere in his wirkyng
He knew ful wel how fer Alnath was shove
Fro the heed of thilke fixe Aries above,
That in the ninthe speere considered is;
Ful subtilly he kalkuled al this.

Whan he hadde founde his firste mansioun,
He knew the remenaunt by proporcioun,
And knew the arisyng of his moone weel,
And in whos face, and terme, and everydeel;
And knew ful weel the moones mansioun
Acordaunt to his operacioun,
And knew also his othere observaunces
For swiche illusiouns and swiche meschaunces
As hethen folk useden in thilke dayes.
For which no lenger maked he delayes,
But thurgh his magik, for a wyke or tweye,
It semed that alle the rokkes were aweye.

Aurelius, which that yet despeired is
Wher he shal han his love or fare amys,
Awaiteth nyght and day on this myracle;
And whan he knew that ther was noon obstacle,
That voyded were thise rokkes everychon,
Doun to his maistres feet he fil anon,
And seyde, 'I woful wrecche, Aurelius,
Thanke yow, lord, and lady myn Venus,
That me han holpen fro my cares colde.'

54

And to the temple his wey forth hath he holde,
Where as he knew he sholde his lady see.
And whan he saugh his tyme, anon-right hee,
With dredful herte and with ful humble cheere,
Salewed hath his sovereyn lady deere:
  'My righte lady,' quod this woful man,
'Whom I moost drede and love as I best kan,
And lothest were of al this world displese,
Nere it that I for yow have swich disese
That I moste dyen heere at youre foot anon,
Noght wolde I telle how me is wo bigon.
But certes outher moste I dye or pleyne;
Ye sle me gilteles for verray peyne.
But of my deeth thogh that ye have no routhe,
Avyseth yow er that ye breke youre trouthe.
Repenteth yow, for thilke God above,
Er ye me sleen by cause that I yow love.
For, madame, wel ye woot what ye han hight –
Nat that I chalange any thyng of right
Of yow, my sovereyn lady, but youre grace –
But in a gardyn yond, at swich a place,
Ye woot right wel what ye bihighten me;
And in myn hand youre trouthe plighten ye
To love me best – God woot, ye seyde so,
Al be that I unworthy am therto.
Madame, I speke it for the honour of yow
Moore than to save myn hertes lyf right now –
I have do so as ye comanded me;
And if ye vouche saf, ye may go see.

Dooth as yow list; have youre biheste in mynde,
For, quyk or deed, right there ye shal me fynde.
In yow lith al to do me lyve or deye –
But wel I woot the rokkes been aweye.'

He taketh his leve, and she astoned stood;
In al hir face nas a drope of blood.
She wende nevere han come in swich a trappe.
'Allas,' quod she, 'that evere this sholde
    happe!
For wende I nevere by possibilitee
That switch a monstre or merveille myghte be!
It is agayns the proces of nature.'
And hoom she goth a sorweful creature;
For verray feere unnethe may she go.
She wepeth, wailleth, al a day or two,
And swowneth, that it routhe was to see.
But why it was to no wight tolde shee,
For out of towne was goon Arveragus.
But to hirself she spak, and seyde thus,
With face pale and with ful sorweful cheere,
In hire compleynt, as ye shall after heere:

    'Allas,' quod she, 'on thee, Fortune, I
        pleyne,
That unwar wrapped hast me in thy cheyne,
Fro which t'escape woot I no socour,
Save oonly deeth or elles dishonour;
Oon of thise two bihoveth me to chese.
But nathelees, yet have I levere to lese
My lif than of my body to have a shame,

56

Or knowe myselven fals, or lese my name;
And with my deth I may be quyt, ywis.
Hath ther nat many a noble wyf er this,
And many a mayde, yslayn hirsel, allas,
Rather than with hir body doon trespas?
'Yis, certes, lo, thise stories beren witnesse:
Whan thritty tirauntz, ful of cursednesse,
Hadde slayn Phidon in Atthenes atte feste,
They comanded his doghtres for t'areste
And bryngen hem biforn hem in despit,
Al naked, to fulfille hir foul delit,
And in hir fadres blood they made hem daunce
Upon the pavement, God yeve hem mes-
    chaunce!
For which thise woful maydens, ful of drede,
Rather than they wolde lese hir maydenhede,
They prively been stirt into a welle
And dreynte hemselven, as the bookes telle.
'They of Mecene leete enquere and seke
Of Lacedomye fifty maydens eke,
On whiche they wolden doon hir lecherye.
But was ther noon of al that compaignye
That she nas slayn, and with a good entente
Chees rather for to dye than assente
To been oppressed of hir maydenhede.
Why sholde I thanne to dye been in drede?
Lo, eek, the tiraunt Aristoclides,
That loved a mayden, heet Stymphalides,
Whan that hir fader slayn was on a nyght,

57

Unto Dianes temple goth she right,
And hente the ymage in hir handes two,
Fro which ymage wolde she nevere go.
No wight ne myghte hir handes of it arace
Til she was slayn, right in the selve place.
    'Now sith that maydens hadden swich despit
To been defouled with mannes foul delit,
Wel oghte a wyf rather hirselven slee
Than be defouled, as it thynketh me.
What shal I seyn of Hasdrubales wyf,
That at Cartage birafte hirself hir lyf?
For whan she saugh that Romayns wan the
    toun,
She took hir children alle, and skipte adoun
Into the fyr, and chees rather to dye
Than any Romayn dide hire vileynye.
Hath nat Lucresse yslayn hirself, allas,
At Rome, whan that she oppressed was
Of Tarquyn, for hire thoughte it was a shame
To lyven whan she hadde lost hir name?
The sevene maydens of Milesie also
Han slayn hemself, for verrey drede and wo,
Rather than folk of Gawle hem sholde oppresse.
Mo than a thousand stories, as I gesse,
Koude I now telle as touchynge this mateere.
Whan Habradate was slayn, his wyf so deere
Hirselven slow, and leet hir blood to glyde
In Habradates woundes depe and wyde,
And seyde, "My body, at the leeste way,

Ther shal no wight defoulen, if I may."
    'What sholde I mo ensamples heerof sayn,
Sith that so manye han hemselven slayn
Wel rather than they wolde defouled be?
I wol conclude that it is bet for me
To sleen myself than been defouled thus.
I wol be trewe unto Arveragus,
Or rather sleen myself in som manere,
As dide Demociones doghter deere
By cause that she wolde nat defouled be.
O Cedasus, it is ful greet pitee
To reden how thy doghtren deyde, allas,
That slowe hemself for swich manere cas.
As greet a pitee was it, or wel moore,
The Theban mayden that for Nichanore
Hirselven slow, right for swich manere wo.
Another Theban mayden dide right so;
For oon of Macidonye hadde hire oppressed,
She with hire deeth hir maydenhede redressed.
What shal I seye of Nicerates wyf,
That for swich cas birafte hirself hir lyf?
How trewe eek was to Alcebiades
His love, that rather for to dyen chees
Than for to suffre his body unburyed be.
Lo, which a wyf was Alceste,' quod she.
'What seith Omer of goode Penalopee?
Al Grece knoweth of hire chastitee.
Pardee, of Laodomya is writen thus,
That whan at Troie was slayn Protheselaus,

Ne lenger wolde she lyve after his day.
The same of noble Porcia telle I may;
Withoute Brutus koude she nat lyve,
To whom she hadde al hool hir herte yive.
The parfit wyfhod of Arthemesie
Honured is thurgh al the Barbarie.
O Teuta, queene, thy wyfly chastitee
To alle wyves may a mirour bee.
The same thyng I seye of Bilyea,
Of Rodogone, and eek Valeria.'

    Thus pleyned Dorigen a day or tweye,
Purposynge evere that she wolde deye.
But nathelees, upon the thridde nyght,
Hoom cam Arveragus, this worthy knyght,
And asked hire why that she weep so soore;
And she gan wepen ever lenger the moore.
'Allas,' quod se, 'that evere was I born!
Thus have I seyd,' quod she, 'thus have I
    sworn' –
And toold hym al as ye han herd bifore;
It nedeth nat reherce it yow namoore.
This housbonde, with glad chiere, in freendly
    wyse
Answerde and seyde as I shal yow devyse:
'Is ther oght elles, Dorigen, but this?'

    'Nay, nay,' quod she, 'God helpe me so as
    wys!
This is to muche, and it were Goddes wille.'
'Ye, wyf,' quod he, 'lat slepen that is stille.

It may be wel, paraventure, yet to day.
Ye shul youre trouthe holden, by my fay!
For God so wisly have mercy upon me,
I hadde wel levere ystiked for to be
For verray love which that I to yow have,
But if ye sholde youre trouthe kepe and save.
Trouthe is the hyeste thyng that man may
    kepe' –
But with that word he brast anon to wepe,
And seyde, 'I yow forbede, up peyne of deeth,
That nevere, whil thee lasteth lyf ne breeth,
To no wight telle thou of this aventure –
As I may best, I wol my wo endure –
Ne make no contenance of hevynesse.
That folk of yow may demen harm or gesse.'

   And forth he cleped a squier and a mayde:
'Gooth forth anon with Dorigen,' he sayde,
'And bryngeth hire to swich a place anon.'
They take hir leve, and on hir wey they gon,
But they ne wiste why she thider wente.
He nolde no wight tellen his entente.

   Paraventure an heep of yow, ywis,
Wol holden hym a lewed man in this
That he wol putte his wyf in jupartie.
Herkneth the tale er ye upon hire crie.
She may have bettre fortune than yow semeth;
And whan that ye han herd the tale, demeth.

   This squier, which that highte Aurelius,
On Dorigen that was so amorus,

Of aventure happed hire to meete
Amydde the toun, right in the quykkest strete,
As she was bown to goon the wey forth right
Toward the gardyn ther as she had hight.
And he was to the gardyn-ward also;
For wel he spyed whan she wolde go
Out of hir hous to any maner place.
But thus they mette, of aventure or grace,
And he saleweth hire with glad entente,
And asked of hire whiderward she wente;
And she answerde, half as she were mad,
'Unto the gardyn, as myn housbonde bad,
My trouthe for to holde – allas, allas!'

    Aurelius gan wondren on this cas,
And in his herte hadde greet compassioun
Of hire and of hire lamentacioun,
And of Arveragus, the worthy knyght,
That bad hire holden al that she had hight,
So looth hym was his wyf sholde breke hir
    trouthe;
And in his herte he caughte of this greet routhe,
Considerynge the beste on every syde,
That fro his lust yet were hym levere abyde
Than doon so heigh a cherlyssh wrecchednesse
Agayns franchise and alle gentillesse;
For which in fewe wordes seyde he thus:

    'Madame, seyth to youre lord Arveragus
That sith I se his grete gentillesse
To yow, and eek I se wel youre distresse,

That him were levere han shame (and that
   were routhe)
Than ye to me sholde breke thus youre trouthe,
I have wel levere evere to suffre wo
Than I departe the love bitwix yow two.
I yow relesse, madame, into youre hond
Quyt every serement and every bond
That ye han maad to me as heerbiforn,
Sith thilke tyme which that ye were born.
My trouthe I plighte, I shal yow never repreve
Of no biheste, and heere I take me leve,
As of the treweste and the beste wyf
That evere yet I knew in al my lyf.
But every wyf be war of hire biheeste!
On Dorigen remembreth, atte leeste.
Thus kan a squire doon a gentil dede
As wel as kan a knyght, withouten drede.'
   She thonketh hym upon hir knees al bare,
And hoom unto hir housbonde is she fare,
And tolde hym al, as ye han herd me sayd;
And be ye siker, he was so weel apayd
That it were impossible me to wryte.
What sholde I lenger of this cas endyte?
   Arveragus and Dorigen his wyf
In sovereyn blisse leden forth hir lyf.
Nevere eft ne was ther agre hem bitwene.
He cherisseth hire as though she were a queene,
And she was to hym trewe for evermoore.
Of thise two folk ye gete of me namoore.

Aurelius, that his cost hath al forlorn,
Curseth the tyme that evere he was born:
'Allas!' quod he. 'Allas, that I bihighte
Of pured gold a thousand pound of wighte
Unto this philosophre! How shal I do?
I se namoore but that I am fordo.
Myn heritage moot I nedes selle,
And been a beggere; heere may I nat dwelle
And shamen al my kynrede in this place,
But I of hym may gete bettre grace.
But nathelees, I wole of hym assaye,
At certeyn dayes, yeer by yeer, to paye,
And thanke hym of his grete curteisye.
My trouthe wol I kepe, I wol nat lye.'

   With herte soor he gooth unto his cofre,
And broghte gold unto this philosophre,
The value of fyve hundred pound, I gesse,
And hym bisecheth, of his gentillesse,
To graunte hym dayes of the remenaunt;
And seyde, 'Maister, I dar el make avaunt,
I failled nevere of my trouthe as yit.
For sikerly my dette shal be quyt
Towardes yow, howevere that I fare
To goon a-begged in my kirtle bare.
But wolde ye vouche sauf, upon seuretee,
Two yeer or thre for to respiten me,
Thanne were I wel; for elles moot I selle
Myn heritage; ther is namoore to telle.'

   This philosophre sobrely answerde,

64

And seyde thus, whan he thise wordes herde:
'Have I nat holden covenant unto thee?'
   'Yes, certes, wel and trewely,' quod he.
   'Hastow nat had thy lady as thee liketh?'
   'No, no,' quod he, and sorwefully he siketh.
   'What was the cause? Tel me if thou kan.'
   Aurelius his tale anon bigan,
And tolde hym al, as ye han herd bifoore;
It nedeth nat to yow reherce it moore.
   He seide, 'Arveragus, of gentillesse,
Hadde levere dye in sorwe and in distresse
Than that his wyf were of hir trouthe fals.'
The sorwe of Dorigen he tolde hym als;
How looth hire was to been a wikked wyf,
And that she levere had lost that day hir lyf,
And that hir trouthe she swoor thurgh innocence
She nevere erst hadde herde speke of apparence.
'That made me han of hire so greet pitee;
And right as frely as he sente hire me,
As frely sente I hire to hym ageyn.
This al and som; ther is namoore to seyn.'
   This philosophre answerde, 'Leeve brother,
Everich of yow dide gentilly til oother.
Thou art a squier, and he is a knyght;
But God forbede, for his blisful myght,
But if a clerk koude doon a gentil dede
As wel as any of yow, it is no drede!
   Sire, I releesse thee thy thousand pound,
As thou right now were cropen out of the

ground,
Ne nevere er now ne haddest knowen me.
For, sire I wol nat taken a peny of thee
For al my craft, ne noght for my travaille.
Thous hast ypayed wel for my vitaille.
It is ynogh, and farewel, have good day!'
And took his hors, and forth he goth his way.
Lordynges, this question, thanne, wol I aske
    now,
Which was the mooste fre, as thynketh yow?
Now telleth me, er that ye ferther wende.
I kan namoore; my tale is at an ende.

I was war of a man in blak,
That sat and had yturned his bak
To an ook, an huge tree.
'Lord,' thoght I, 'who may that be?
What ayleth hym to sitten her?'
Anoon-ryght I wente ner;
Than found I sitte even upryght
A wonder wel-farynge knyght –
By the maner me thoghte so –
Of good mochel, and ryght yong therto,
Of the age of foure and twenty yer,
Upon hys berd but lytel her,
And he was clothed al in blak.
I stalked even unto hys bak,
And there I stood as stille as ought,
That, soth to saye, he saw me nought;
For-why he heng hys hed adoun,
And with a dedly sorwful soun
He made of rym ten vers or twelve
Of a compleynte to hymselve –
The moste pitee, the moste rowthe,
That ever I herde; for, by my trowthe,
Hit was gret wonder that Nature
Myght suffre any creature
To have such sorwe and be not ded.
Ful pitous pale and nothyng red,

He sayd a lay, a maner song,
Withoute noote, withoute song;
And was thys, for ful wel I kan
Reherse hyt; ryght thus hyt began:

  'I have of sorwe so gret won
That joye gete I never non,
Now that I see my lady bryght,
Which I have loved with al my myght,
Is fro me ded and ys agoon.
'Allas, deth, what ayleth the,
That thou noldest have taken me,
Whan thou toke my lady swete,
That was so fair, so fresh, so fre,
So good that men may wel se
Of al goodnesse she had no mete!'

  Whan he had mad thus his complaynte,
Hys sorwful hert gan faste faynte
And his spirites wexen dede;
The blood was fled for pure drede
Doun to hys herte, to make hym warm –
For wel hyt feled the herte had harm –
To wite eke why hyt was adrad
By kynde, and for to make hyt glad,
For hit ys membre principal
Of the body; and that made al
Hys hewe chaunge and wexe grene
And pale, for ther noo blood ys sene
In no maner lym of hys.

Anoon therwith whan y sawgh this –
He ferde thus evel there he set –
I went and stood ryght at his fet,
And grette hym; but he spak noght,
But argued with his owne thoght,
And in hys wyt disputed faste
Why and how hys lyf myght laste;
Hym thoughte hys sorwes were so smerte
And lay so colde upon hys herte.
So, throgh hys sorwe and hevy thoght,
Made hym that he herde me noght;
For he had wel nygh lost hys mynde,
Thogh Pan, that men clepeth god of kynde,
Were for hys sorwes never so wroth.

But at the last, to sayn ryght soth,
He was war of me, how y stood
Before hym and did of myn hood,
And had ygret hym as I best koude,
Debonayrly, and nothyng lowde.
He sayde, 'I prey the, be not wroth.
I herde the not, to seyn the soth,
Ne I sawgh the not, syr, trewely.'

'A, goode sir, no fors,' quod y,
'I am ryght sory yif I have ought
Destroubled yow out of your thought.
Foryive me, yif I have mystake.'

'Yis, th'amendes is lyght to make,'
Quod he, 'for ther lyeth noon therto;
There ys nothyng myssayd nor do.'

69

Whan I was fro thys egle goon,
I gan beholde upon this place.
And certein, or I ferther pace,
I wol yow al the shap devyse
Of hous and site, and al the wyse
How I gan to thys place aproche
That stood upon so hygh a roche,
Hier stant ther non in Spayne.
But up I clomb with alle payne,
And though to clymbe it greved me,
Yit I ententyf was to see,
And for to powren wonder lowe,
Yf I koude any weyes knowe
What maner stoon this roche was.
For hyt was lyk alum de glas,
But that hyt shoon ful more clere;
But of what congeled matere
Hyt was, I nyste redely.
But at the laste aspied I,
And found that hit was every del
A roche of yse, and not of stel.
Thoughte I, 'By Seynt Thomas of Kent,
This were a feble fundament
To bilden on a place hye.
He ought him lytel glorifye
That hereon bilt, God so me save!'
   Tho sawgh I al the half ygrave

With famous folkes names fele,
That had iben in mochel wele,
And her fames wide yblowe.
But wel unnethes koude I knowe
Any lettres for to rede
Hir names by; for, out of drede,
They were almost ofthowed so
That of the lettres oon or two
Was molte away of every name,
So unfamous was woxe hir fame.
But men seyn, 'What may ever laste?'

   Thoo gan I in myn herte caste
That they were molte awey with hete,
And not awey with stormes bete.
For on that other syde I say
Of this hil, that northward lay,
How hit was writen ful of names
Of folkes that hadden grete fames
Of olde tyme, and yet they were
As fressh as men had writen hem here
The selve day ryght, or that houre
That I upon hem gan to poure.
But wel I wiste what yt made;
Hyt was conserved with the shade
Of a castel that stood on high –
Al this writynge that I sigh –
And stood eke on so cold a place
That hete myghte hit not deface.

Thoo gan I up the hil to goon,
And fond upon the cop a woon,
That al the men that ben on lyve
Ne han the kunnynge to descrive
The beaute of that ylke place,
Ne coude casten no compace
Swich another for to make,
That myght of beaute ben hys make,
Ne so wonderlych ywrought;
That hit astonyeth yit my thought,
And maketh al my wyt to swynke,
On this castel to bethynke,
So that the grete craft, beaute,
The cast, the curiosite
Ne kan I not to yow devyse;
My wit ne may me not suffise.
    But natheles al the substance
I have yit in my remembrance;
For whi me thoughte, be Seynt Gyle,
Al was of ston of beryle,
Bothe the castel and the tour,
And eke the halle and every bour,
Wythouten peces or joynynges.
But many subtil compassinges,
Babewynnes and pynacles,
Ymageries and tabernacles
I say; and ful eke of wyndowes
As flakes falle in grete snowes.

And eke in ech of the pynacles
Weren sondry habitacles,
In which stoden, al withoute –
Ful the castel, al aboute –
Of alle maner of mynstralles
And gestiours that tellen tales
Both of wepinge and of game,
Of al that longeth unto Fame.

From THE PARLIAMENT OF FOWLS

The lyf so short, the craft so long to lerne,
Th'assay so hard, so sharp the conquerynge,
The dredful joye alwey that slit so yerne:
Al this mene I by Love, that my felynge
Astonyeth with his wonderful werkynge
So sore, iwis, that whan I on hym thynke
Nat wot I wel wher that I flete or synke.

For al be that I knowe nat Love in dede,
Ne wot how that he quiteth folk here *hyre*,
Yit happeth me ful ofte in bokes reede
Of his myrakles and his crewel yre.
There rede I wel he wol be lord and syre;
I dar nat seyn, his strokes been so sore,
But 'God save swich a lord!' – I can na moore.

Of usage – what for lust and what for lore –
On bokes rede I ofte, as I yow tolde.
But wherfore that I speke al this? Nat yoore
Agon it happede me for to beholde
Upon a bok, was write with lettres olde,
And therupon, a certeyn thing to lerne,
The longe day ful faste I redde and yerne.

For out of olde feldes, as men seyth,
Cometh al this newe corn from yer to yere,
And out of olde bokes, in good feyth,
Cometh al this newe science that men lere.
But now to purpos as of this matere:
To rede forth hit gan me so delite
That al that day me thoughte but a lyte.

This bok of which I make mencioun
Entitled was al ther, as I shal telle:
'Tullyus of the Drem of Scipioun.'
Chapitres sevene it hadde, of hevene and helle
And erthe, and soules that therinne dwelle,
Of whiche, as shortly as I can it trete,
Of his sentence I wol yow seyn the greete.

A gardyn saw I ful of blosmy bowes
Upon a ryver, in a grene mede,
There as swetnesse everemore inow is,
With flours white, blewe, yelwe, and rede,
And colde welle-stremes, nothyng dede,
That swymmen ful of smale fishes lighte,
With fynnes rede and skales sylver bryghte.

On every bow the bryddes herde I synge,
With voys of aungel in here armonye;
Some besyede hem here bryddes forth to brynge;
The litel conyes to here pley gonne hye;
And ferther al aboute I gan aspye
The dredful ro, the buk, the hert and hynde,
Squyrels, and bestes smale of gentil kynde.

Of instruments of strenges in acord
Herde I so pleye a ravyshyng swetnesse,
That God, that makere is of al and lord,
Ne herde nevere beter, as I gesse.
Therwith a wynd, unnethe it myghte be lesse,
Made in the leves grene a noyse softe
Acordaunt to the foules song alofte.

Th'air of that place so attempre was
That nevere was grevaunce of hot ne cold.
There wex ek every holsom spice and gras;
No man may there waxe sek ne old;
Yit was there joye more a thousandfold
Than man can telle; ne nevere wolde it nyghte,
But ay cler day to any mannes syghte.

Under a tre, besyde a welle, I say
Cupide, oure lord, his arwes forge and file;
And at his fet his bowe al redy lay;
And Wille, his doughter, temprede al this while
The hevedes in the welle, and with hire wile
She couchede hem, after they shulde serve
Some for to sle, and some to wounde and kerve.

Tho was I war of Plesaunce anon-ryght,
And of Aray, and Lust, and Curteysie,
And of the Craft that can and hath the myght
To don by force a wyght to don folye –
Disfigurat was she, I nyl nat lye;
And by hymself, under an ok, I gesse,
Saw I Delyt, that stod with Gentilesse.

I saw Beute withouten any atyr,
And Youthe, ful of game and jolyte;
Foolhardynesse, Flaterye, and Desyr,
Messagerye, and Meede, and other thre –
Here names shul not here be told for me –
And upon pilers greete of jasper longe
I saw a temple of bras ifounded stronge.

Aboute the temple daunsedyn alwey
Women inowe, of whiche some ther weere
Fayre of hemself, and some of hem were gay.
In kertels, al dishevele, wente they there:
That was here offyce alwey, yer by yeere.
And on the temple, of dowves white and fayre
Saw I syttynge many an hundred peyre.

Byfore the temple-dore ful soberly
Dame Pees sat, with a curtyn in hire hond,
And by hire syde, wonder discretly,
Dame Pacience syttynge there I fond,
With face pale, upon an hil of sond;
And aldernext, withinne and ek withoute,
Byheste and Art, and of here folk a route.

Withinne the temple, of sykes hoote as fyr
I herde a swogh that gan aboute renne,
Whiche sikes were engendered with desyr,
That maden every auter for to brenne
Of newe flaume; and wel espyed I thenne
That al the cause of sorwes that they drye
Cam of the bittere goddesse Jelosye.

The god Priapus saw I, as I wente,
Withinne the temple in sovereyn place stonde,
In swich aray as whan the asse hym shente
With cri by nighte, and with hys sceptre in honde.
Ful besyly men gonne assaye and fonde
Upon his hed to sette, of sondry hewe,
Garlondes ful of freshe floures newe.

And in a prive corner in disport
Fond I Venus and hire porter Richesse,
That was ful noble and hautayn of hyre port
Derk was that place, but afterward lightnesse
I saw a lyte, unnethe it myghte be lesse –
And on a bed of gold she lay to reste,
Til that the hote sonne gan to weste.

Hyre gilte heres with a golden thred
Ibounden were, untressed as she lay,
And naked from the brest unto the hed
Men myghte hire sen; and, sothly for to say,
The remenaunt was wel kevered to my pay,
Ryght with a subtyl coverchef of Valence –
Ther was no thikkere cloth of no defense.

The place yaf a thousand savours sote,
And Bachus, god of wyn, sat hire besyde,
And Ceres next, that doth of hunger boote,
And, as I seyde, amyddes lay Cypride,
To whom on knees two yonge folk ther cryde
To ben here helpe. But thus I let hire lye,
And ferther in the temple I gan espie

That, in dispit of Dyane the chaste,
Ful many a bowe ibroke heng on the wal
Of maydenes swiche as gonne here tymes waste
In hyre servyse; and peynted overal
Ful many a story, of which I touche shal
A fewe, as of Calyxte and Athalante,
And many a mayde of which the name I wante.

Semyramis, Candace, and Hercules,
Biblis, Dido, Thisbe, and Piramus,
Tristram, Isaude, Paris, and Achilles,
Eleyne, Cleopatre, and Troylus,
Silla, and ek the moder of Romulus:
Alle these were peynted on that other syde,
And al here love, and in what plyt they dyde.

Whan I was come ayeyn into the place
That I of spak, that was so sote and grene,
Forth welk I tho myselven to solace.
Tho was I war wher that ther sat a queene
That, as of lyght the somer sonne shene
Passeth the sterre, right so over mesure
She fayrer was than any creature.

And in a launde, upon an hil of floures,
Was set this noble goddesse Nature.
Of braunches were here halles and here boures
Iwrought after here cast and here mesure;
Ne there nas foul that cometh of engendrure
That they ne were prest in here presence
To take hire dom and yeve hire audyence.

For this was on Seynt Valentynes day,
Whan every foul cometh there to chese his make,
Of every kynde that men thynke may,
And that so huge a noyse gan they make
That erthe, and eyr, and tre, and every lake
So ful was that unethe was there space
For me to stonde, so ful was al the place.

And right as Aleyn, in the Pleynt of Kynde,
Devyseth Nature of aray and face,
In swich aray men myghte hire there fynde.
This noble emperesse, ful of grace,
Bad every foul to take his owne place,
As they were woned alwey fro yer to yeere,
Seynt Valentynes day, to stonden theere.

That is to seyn, the foules of ravyne
Weere hyest set, and thanne the foules smale
That eten, as hem Nature wolde enclyne,
As worm or thyng of which I telle no tale;
And water-foul sat lowest in the dale;
But foul that lyveth by sed sat on the grene,
And that so fele that wonder was to sene.

There myghte men the royal egle fynde,
That with his sharpe lok perseth the sonne,
And othere egles of a lowere kynde,
Of whiche that clerkes wel devyse conne.
Ther was the tiraunt with his fetheres donne
And grey – I mene the goshauk that doth pyne
To bryddes for his outrageous ravyne.

The gentyl faucoun, that with his feet distrayneth
The kynges hand; the hardy sperhauk eke,
The quayles foo; the merlioun, that payneth
Hymself ful ofte the larke for to seke;
There was the douve with hire yĕn meke;
The jelous swan, ayens his deth that syngeth;
The oule ek, that of deth the bode bryngeth;

The crane, the geaunt, with his trompes soun;
The thef, the chough; and ek the janglynge pye;
The skornynge jay; the eles fo, heroun;
The false lapwynge, ful of trecherye;
The stare, that the conseyl can bewrye;
The tame ruddok, and the coward kyte;
The kok, that orloge is of thorpes lyte;

The sparwe, Venus sone; the nyghtyngale,
That clepeth forth the grene leves newe;
The swalwe, mortherere of the foules smale
That maken hony of floures freshe of hewe;
The wedded turtil, with hire herte trewe;
The pekok, with his aungels fetheres bryghte;
The fesaunt, skornere of the cok by nyghte;

The waker goos; the cukkow ever unkynde;
The popynjay, ful of delicasye;
The drake, stroyere of his owene kynde;
The stork, the wrekere of avouterye;
The hote cormeraunt of glotenye;
The raven wys; the crowe with vois of care;
The throstil old; the frosty feldefare.

What shulde I seyn? Of foules every kynde
That in this world han fetheres and stature
Men myghten in that place assembled fynde
Byfore the noble goddesse Nature,
And ech of hem dide his besy cure
Benygnely to chese or for to take,
By hire acord, his formel or his make.

From TROILUS AND CRISEYDE

Book 1

The double sorwe of Troilus to tellen,
That was the kyng Priamus sone of Troye,
In lovynge, how his aventures fellen
Fro wo to wele, and after out of joie,
My purpos is, er that I parte fro ye.
Thesiphone, thow help me for t'endite
Thise woful vers, that wepen as I write.

To the clepe I, thow goddesse of torment,
Thow cruwel Furie, sorwynge evere in peyne,
Help me, that am the sorwful instrument,
That helpeth loveres, as I kan, to pleyne;
For wel sit it, the sothe for to seyne,
A woful wight to han a drery feere,
And to a sorwful tale, a sory chere.

For I, that God of Loves servantz serve,
Ne dar to Love, for myn unliklynesse,
Preyen for speed, al sholde I therfore sterve,
So fer am I from his help in derknesse.
But natheles, if this may don gladnesse
Unto any lovere, and his cause availle,
Have he my thonk, and myn be this travaille!

But ye loveres, that bathen in gladnesse,
If any drope of pyte in yow be,
Remembreth yow on passed hevynesse
That ye han felt, and on the adversite
Of othere folk, and thynketh how that ye
Han felt that Love dorste yow displese,
Or ye han wonne hym with to gret an ese.

And preieth for hem that ben in the cas
Of Troilus, as ye may after here,
That Love hem brynge in hevene to solas;
And ek for me preieth to God so dere
That I have myght to shewe, in som manere,
Swich peyne and wo as Loves folk endure,
In Troilus unsely aventure.

And biddeth ek for hem that ben despeired
In love, that nevere nyl recovered be,
And ek for hem that falsly ben apeired
Thorugh wikked tonges, be it he or she;
Thus biddeth God, for his benignite,
So graunte hem soone owt of this world to pace,
That ben despeired out of Loves grace.

And biddeth ek for hem that ben at ese,
That God hem graunte ay good perseveraunce,
And sende hem myght hire ladies so to plese
That it to Love be worship and plesaunce.
For so hope I my sowle best avaunce,
To prey for hem that Loves servauntz be,
And write hire wo, and lyve in charite,

And for to have of hem compassioun,
As though I were hire owne brother dere.
Now herkneth with a good entencioun,
For now wil I gon streght to my matere,
In which ye may the double sorwes here
Of Troilus in lovynge of Criseyde,
And how that she forsook hym er she deyde.

So ferde it by this fierse and proude knyght:
Though he a worthy kynges sone were,
And wende nothing hadde had swich myght
Ayeyns his wille that shuld his herte stere,
Yet with a look his herte wex a-fere,
That he that now was moost in pride above,
Wax sodeynly moost subgit unto love.

'I have herd told, pardieux, of youre lyvynge,
Ye loveres, and youre lewed observaunces,
And which a labour folk han in wynnynge
Of love, and in the kepyng which doutaunces;
And whan youre prey is lost, woo and penaunces.
O veray fooles, nyce and blynde be ye!
Ther nys nat oon kan war by other be.'

And with that word he gan caste up the browe,
Ascaunces, 'Loo! is this naught wisely spoken?'
At which the God of Love gan loken rowe
Right for despit, and shop for to ben wroken.
He kidde anon his bowe nas naught broken;
For sodeynly he hitte hym atte fulle –
And yet as proud a pekok kan he pulle.

O blynde world, O blynde entencioun!
How often falleth al the effect contraire
Of surquidrie and foul presumpcioun;
For kaught is proud, and kaught is debonaire.
This Troilus is clomben on the staire,
And litel weneth that he moot descenden;
But alday faileth thing that fooles wenden.

As proude Bayard gynneth for to skippe
Out of the weye, so pryketh hym his corn,
Til he a lasshe have of the longe whippe –
Than thynketh he, 'Though I praunce al byforn
First in the trays, ful fat and newe shorn,
Yet am I but an hors, and horses lawe
I moot endure, and with my feres drawe' –

Forthy ensample taketh of this man,
Ye wise, proude, and worthi folkes alle,
To scornen Love, which that so soone kan
The fredom of youre hertes to hym thralle;
For evere it was, and evere it shal byfalle,
That Love is he that alle thing may bynde,
For may no man fordon the lawe of kynde.

That this be soth, hath preved and doth yit.
For this trowe I ye knowen alle or some,
Men reden nat that folk han gretter wit
Than they that han be most with love ynome;
And strengest folk ben therwith overcome,
The worthiest and grettest of degree:
This was, and is, and yet men shall it see.

And trewelich it sit wel to be so,
For alderwisest han therwith ben plesed;
And they that han ben aldermost in wo,
With love han ben comforted moost and esed;
And ofte it hath the cruel herte apesed,
And worthi folk maad worthier of name,
And causeth moost to dreden vice and shame.

Now sith it may nat goodly ben withstonde,
And is a thing so vertuous in kynde,
Refuseth nat to Love for to ben bonde,
Syn, as hymselven liste, he may yow bynde;
The yerde is bet that bowen wole and wynde
Than that that brest, and therfore I yow rede
To folowen hym that so wel kan yow lede.

But for to tellen forth in special
Of this kynges sone of which I tolde,
And leten other thing collateral,
Of hym thenke I my tale forth to holde,
Both of his joie and of his cares colde;
And al his werk, as touching this matere,
For I it gan, I wol therto refere.

Withinne the temple he wente hym forth pleyinge,
This Troilus, of every wight aboute,
On this lady, and now on that, lokynge,
Wher so she were of town or of withoute;
And upon cas bifel that thorugh a route
His eye percede, and so depe it wente,
Til on Criseyde it smot, and ther it stente.

And sodeynly he wax therwith astoned,
And gan hir bet biholde in thrifty wise.
'O mercy, God,' thoughte he, 'wher hastow woned,
That art so feyr and goodly to devise?'
Therwith his herte gan to sprede and rise,
And softe sighed, lest men myghte hym here,
And caught ayeyn his firste pleyinge chere.

She nas nat with the leste of hire stature,
But alle hire lymes so wel answerynge
Weren to wommanhod, that creature
Was nevere lasse mannyssh in semynge;
And ek the pure wise of hire mevynge
Shewed wel that men myght in hire gesse
Honour, estat, and wommanly noblesse.

To Troilus right wonder wel with alle
Gan for to like hire mevynge and hire chere,
Which somdel deignous was, for she let falle
Hire look a lite aside in swich manere,
Ascaunces, 'What, may I nat stonden here?'
And after that hir lokynge gan she lighte,
That nevere thoughte hym seen so good a syghte.

And of hire look in him ther gan to quyken
So gret desir and such affeccioun,
That in his herte botme gan to stiken
Of hir his fixe and depe impressioun.
And though he erst hadde poured up and down,
He was tho glad his hornes in to shrinke:
Unnethes wiste he how to loke or wynke.

Lo, he that *leet* hymselven so konnynge,
And scorned hem that Loves peynes dryen,
Was ful unwar that Love hadde his dwellynge
Withinne the subtile stremes of hire yen;
That sodeynly hym thoughte he felte dyen,
Right with hire look, the spirit in his herte:
Blissed be Love, that kan thus folk converte!

Book 3

So whan that she was in the closet leyd,
And alle hire wommen forth by ordinaunce
Abedde weren, ther as I have seyd,
Ther was nomore to skippen nor to traunce,
But boden go to bedde, with meschaunce,
If any wight was steryng anywhere,
And lat hem slepen that abedde were.

But Pandarus, that wel koude ech a deel
Th'olde daunce, and every point therinne,
Whan that he sey that alle thyng was wel,
He thought he wolde upon his werk bigynne,
And gan the stuwe doore al softe unpynne;
And stille as stoon, withouten lenger lette,
By Troilus adown right he hym sette,

And shortly to the point right for to gon,
Of al this werk he tolde hym word and ende,
And seyde, 'Make the redy right anon,
For thow shalt into hevene blisse wende.'
'Now, blisful Venus, thow me grace sende!'
Quod Troilus, 'For nevere yet no nede
Hadde ich er now, ne halvendel the drede.'

Quod Pandarus, 'Ne drede the nevere a deel,
For it shal be right as thow wolt desire;
So thryve I, this nyght shal I make it weel,
Or casten al the gruwel in the fire.'
'Yet, blisful Venus, this nyght thow me enspire,'
Quod Troilus, 'As wys as I the serve,
And evere bet and bet shal, til I sterve.

'And if ich hadde, O Venus ful of myrthe,
Aspectes badde of Mars or of Saturne,
Or thow combust or let were in my birthe,
Thy fader prey al thilke harm disturne
Of grace, and that I glad ayein may turne,
For love of hym thow lovedest in the shawe –
I meene Adoun, that with the boor was slawe.

'O Jove ek, for the love of faire Europe,
The which in forme of bole awey thow fette,
Now help! O Mars, thow with thi blody cope,
For love of Cipris, thow me nought ne lette!
O Phebus, thynk whan Dane hireselven shette
Under the bark, and laurer wax for drede;
Yet for hire love, O help now at this nede!

94

'Mercurie, for the love of Hierse eke,
For which Pallas was with Aglawros wroth,
Now help! And ek Diane, I the biseke
That this viage be nought to the looth!
O fatal sustren which, er any cloth
Me shapen was, my destine me sponne,
So helpeth to this werk that is bygonne!'

Quod Pandarus, 'Thow wrecched mouses herte,
Artow agast so that she wol the bite?
Wy! Don this furred cloke upon thy sherte,
And folwe me, for I wol have the wite.
But bid, and lat me gon biforn a lite.'
And with that word he gan undon a trappe,
And Troilus he brought in by the lappe.

The sterne wynd so loude gan to route
That no wight oother noise myghte heere;
And they that layen at the dore withoute,
Ful sikerly they slepten alle yfere;
And Pandarus, with a ful sobre cheere,
Goth to the dore anon, withouten lette,
Ther as they laye, and softely it shette.

And as he com ayeynward pryvely,
His nece awook, and axed, 'Who goth there?'
'My dere nece,' quod he, 'it am I.
Ne wondreth nought, ne have of it no fere.'
And ner he com and seyde hire in hire ere,
'No word, for love of God, I yow biseche!
Lat no wight risen and heren of oure speche.'

'What, which wey be ye comen, benedicite?'
Quod she; 'And how, unwist of hem alle?'
'Here at this secre trappe-dore,' quod he.
Quod tho Criseyde, 'Lat me som wight calle!'
'I! God forbede that it sholde falle,'
Quod Pandarus, 'that ye swich folye wroughte!
They myghte demen thyng they nevere er thoughte.

'It is nought good a slepyng hound to wake,
Ne yeve a wight a cause to devyne:
Youre wommen slepen alle, I undertake,
So that, for hem, the hous men myghte myne,
And slepen wollen til the sonne shyne.
And whan my tale brought is to an ende,
Unwist, right as I com, so wol I wende.

'Now, nece myn, ye shul wel understonde,'
Quod he, 'so as ye wommen demen alle,
That for to holde in love a man in honde,
And hym hire lief and deere herte calle,
And maken hym an howve above a calle –
I meene, as love another in this while –
She doth hireself a shame and hym a gyle.

'Now, wherby that I telle yow al this:
Ye woot yourself, as wel as any wight,
How that youre love al fully graunted is
To Troilus, the worthieste knyght,
Oon of this world, and therto trouthe yplight,
That, but it were on hym along, ye nolde
Hym nevere falsen while ye lyven sholde.

'Now stant it thus, that sith I fro yow wente,
This Troilus, right platly for to seyn,
Is through a goter, by a pryve wente,
Into my chaumbre come in al this reyn,
Unwist of every manere wight, certeyn,
Save of myself, as wisly have I joye,
And by that feith I shal Priam of Troie.

'And he is come in swich peyne and distresse
That, but he be al fully wood by this,
He sodeynly mot falle into wodnesse,
But if God helpe; and cause whi this is:
He seith hym told is of a frend of his,
How that ye sholden love oon hatte Horaste;
For sorwe of which this nyght shal ben his laste.'

Criseyde, which that al this wonder herde,
Gan sodeynly aboute hire herte colde,
And with a sik she sorwfully answerde,
'Allas! I wende, whoso tales tolde,
My deere herte wolde me nought holde
So lightly fals! Allas, conceytes wronge,
What harm they don! For now lyve I to longe!

'Horaste! Allas, and falsen Troilus?
I knowe hym nought, God helpe me so!' quod she.
'Allas, what wikked spirit tolde hym thus?
Now certes, em, tomorwe and I hym se,
I shal therof as ful excusen me,
As evere dide womman, if hym like.'
And with that word she gan ful soore sike.

'O God,' quod she, 'so worldly *selynesse*,
Which clerkes callen fals felicitee,
Imedled is with many a bitternesse!
Ful angwissous than is, God woot,' quod she,
'Condicioun of veyn prosperitee:
For either joies comen nought yfeere,
Or elles no wight hath hem alwey here.

'O brotel wele of mannes joie unstable!
With what wight so thow be, or how thow pleye,
Either he woot that thow, joie art muable,
Or woot it nought; it mot ben oon of tweye.
Now if he woot it nought, how may he seye
That he hath verray joie and selynesse,
That is of ignoraunce ay in derknesse?

'Now if he woot that joie is transitorie,
As every joye of worldly thyng mot flee,
Than every tyme he that hath in memorie,
The drede of lesyng maketh hym that he
May in no perfit selynesse be;
And if to lese his joie he sette a myte,
Than semeth it that joie is worth ful lite.

'Wherfore I wol diffyne in this matere,
That trewely, for aught I kan espie,
Ther is no verray weele in this world heere.
But O thow wikked serpent, jalousie,
Thow mysbyleved envyous folie,
Why hastow Troilus mad to me untriste,
That nevere yet agylte hym, that I wiste?'

Quod Pandarus, 'Thus fallen is this cas –'
'Wy! Uncle myn,' quod she, 'who tolde hym this?
Why doth my deere herte thus, allas?'
'Ye woot, ye, nece myn,' quod he, 'what is.
I hope al shal be wel that is amys,
For ye may quenche al this, if that yow leste –
And doth right so, for I holde it the beste.'

'So shal I do to-morwe, ywys,' quod she,
'And God toforn, so that it shal suffise.'
'To-morwe? Allas, that were a fair!' quod he;
'Nay, nay, it may nat stonden in this wise,
For, nece myn, thus writen clerkes wise,
That peril is with drecchyng in ydrawe;
Nay, swiche abodes ben nought worth an hawe.

'Nece, alle thyng hath tyme, I dar avowe;
For whan a chaumbre afire is or an halle,
Wel more nede is, it sodeynly rescowe
Than to dispute and axe amonges alle
How this candel in the strawe is falle.
A, benedicite! For al among that fare
The harm is don, and fare-wel feldefare!

'And nece myn – ne take it naught agrief
If that ye suffre hym al nyght in this wo,
God help me so, ye hadde hym nevere lief!
That dar I seyn, now ther is but we two.
But wel I woot that ye wol nat do so;
Ye ben to wys to doon so gret folie,
To putte his lif al nyght in jupertie.'

'Hadde I hym nevere lief? by God, I weene
Ye hadde nevere thyng so lief!' quod she.
'Now by my thrift,' quod he, 'that shal be seene!
For syn ye make this ensaumple of me,
If ich al nyght wolde hym in sorwe se,
For al the tresour in the town of Troie,
I bidde God I nevere mote have joie.

'Now loke thanne, if ye that ben his love
Shul putte his lif al night in jupertie
For thyng of nought, now by that God above,
Naught oonly this delay comth of folie,
But of malice, if that I shal naught lie.
What! Platly, and ye suffre hym in destresse,
Ye neyther bounte don ne gentilesse.'

Quod tho Criseyde, 'Wol ye don o thyng
And ye therwith shal stynte al his disese?
Have heere, and bereth hym this blewe ryng,
For ther is nothyng myghte hym bettre plese,
Save I myself, ne more hys herte apese;
And sey my deere herte that his sorwe
Is causeles; that shal be sene to-morwe.'

'A ryng?' quod he, 'Ye haselwodes shaken!
Ye, nece myn, that ryng moste han a stoon
That myghte dede men alyve maken;
And swich a ryng trowe I that ye have non.
Discrecioun out of youre hed is gon;
That fele I now,' quod he, 'and that is routhe.
O tyme ilost, wel maistow corsen slouthe!

'Woot ye not wel that noble and heigh corage
Ne sorweth nought, ne stynteth ek, for lite?
But if a fool were in a jalous rage,
I nolde setten at his sorwe a myte,
But feffe hym with a fewe wordes white
Anothir day, whan that I myghte hym fynde;
But this thyng stant al in another kynde.

'This is so gentil and so tendre of herte
That with his deth he wol his sorwes wreke;
For trusteth wel, how sore that hym smerte,
He wol to yow no jalous wordes speke.
And forthi, nece, er that his herte breke,
So speke yourself to hym of this matere,
For with o word ye may his herte stere.

'Now have I told what peril he is inne,
And his comynge unwist is to every wight;
Ne, parde, harm may ther be non, ne synne:
I wol myself be with yow al this nyght.
Ye knowe ek how it is youre owen knyght,
And that bi right ye moste upon hym triste,
And I al prest to fecche hym whan yow liste.'

This accident so pitous was to here,
And ek so like a sooth at prime face,
And Troilus hire knyght to hir so deere,
His prive comyng, and the siker place,
That though that she did hym as thanne a grace,
Considered alle thynges as they stoode,
No wonder is, syn she did al for goode.

Criseyde answerde, 'As wisly God at reste
My soule brynge, as me is for hym wo!
And em, iwis, fayn wolde I don the beste,
If that ich hadde grace to do so;
But whether that ye dwelle or for hym go,
I am, til God me bettre mynde sende,
At dulcarnoun, right at my wittes ende.'

Quod Pandarus, 'Yee, nece, wol ye here?
Dulcarnoun called is "flemyng of wrecches":
It semeth hard, for wrecches wol nought lere,
For verray slouthe or other wilfull tecches;
This seyd by hem that ben nought worth two fecches;
But ye ben wis, and that we han on honde
Nis neither hard, ne skilful to withstonde.'

'Than, em,' quod she, 'doth herof as yow list.
But er he com, I wil up first arise,
And for the love of God, syn al my trist
Is on yow two, and ye ben bothe wise,
So werketh now in so discret a wise
That I honour may have, and he plesaunce
For I am here al in youre governaunce.'

'That is wel seyd,' quod he, 'my nece deere
Ther good thrift on that wise gentil herte
But liggeth stille, and taketh hym right here –
It nedeth nought no ferther for hym sterte
And ech of yow ese otheres sorwes smerte.
For love of God! And Venus, I the herye,
For soone hope I we shul ben alle merye.'

This Troilus ful soone on knees hym sette
Ful sobrely, right be hyre beddes hed,
And in his beste wyse his lady grette.
But Lord, so she wex sodeynliche red!
Ne though men sholde smyten of hire hed,
She kouthe nought a word aright out brynge
So sodeynly, for his sodeyn comynge.

But Pandarus, that so wel koude feele
In every thyng, to pleye anon bigan,
And seyde, 'Nece, se how this lord kan knele!
Now for youre trouthe, se this gentil man!'
And with that word he for a quysshen ran,
And seyde, 'Kneleth now, while that yow leste;
There God youre hertes brynge soone at reste!'

Kan I naught seyn, for she bad hym nought rise,
If sorwe it putte out of hire remembraunce,
Or elles that she took it in the wise
Of dewete, as for his observaunce;
But wel fynde I she dede hym this plesaunce,
That she hym kiste, although she siked sore,
And bad hym sitte adown withouten more.

Quod Pandarus, 'Now wol ye wel bigynne.
Now doth hym sitte, goode nece deere,
Upon youre beddes syde al ther withinne,
That ech of yow the bet may other heere.'

From THE LEGEND OF GOOD WOMEN

A thousand tymes have I herd men telle
That ther ys joy in hevene and peyne in helle,
And I acorde wel that it ys so;
But, natheles, yet wot I wel also
That ther nis noon dwellyng in this contree
That eyther hath in hevene or helle ybe,
Ne may of hit noon other weyes witen
But as he hath herd seyd or founde it writen;
For by assay ther may no man it preve.
But God forbede but men shulde leve
Wel more thing then men han seen with ye!
Men shal not wenen every thing a lye
But yf himself yt seeth or elles dooth;
For, God wot, thing is never the lasse sooth,
Thogh every wight ne may it nat ysee.
Bernard the monk ne saugh nat all, pardee!
    Than mote we to bokes that we fynde,
Thurgh whiche that olde thinges ben in mynde,
And to the doctrine of these olde wyse,
Yeve credence, in every skylful wise,
That tellen of these olde appreved stories
Of holynesse, of regnes, of victories,
Of love, of hate, of other sondry thynges,
Of whiche I may not maken rehersynges.
And yf that olde bokes were aweye,
Yloren were of remembraunce the keye.

Wel ought us thanne honouren and beleve
These bokes, there we han noon other preve.

   And as for me, though that I konne but lyte,
On bokes for to rede I me delyte,
And to hem yive I feyth and ful credence,
And in myn herte have hem in reverence
So hertely, that ther is game noon
That fro my bokes maketh me to goon,
But yt be seldom on the holyday,
Save, certeynly, whan that the month of May
Is comen, and that I here the foules synge,
And that the floures gynnen for to sprynge,
Farewel my bok and my devocioun!

   Now have I thanne eek this condicioun,
That, of al the floures in the mede,
Thanne love I most thise floures white and rede,
Swiche as men callen daysyes in our toun.
To hem have I so gret affeccioun,
As I seyde erst, whanne comen is the May,
That in my bed ther daweth me no day
That I nam up and walkyng in the mede
To seen this flour ayein the sonne sprede,
Whan it upryseth erly by the morwe.
That blisful sighte softneth al my sorwe,
So glad am I, whan that I have presence
Of it, to doon it alle reverence,
As she that is of alle floures flour,
Fulfilled of al vertu and honour,

And evere ilyke faire and fressh of hewe;
And I love it, and ever ylike newe,
And evere shal, til that myn herte dye.
Al swere I nat, of this I wol nat lye;
Ther loved no wight hotter in his lyve.
And whan that hit ys eve, I renne blyve,
As sone as evere the sonne gynneth weste,
To seen this flour, how it wol go to reste,
For fere of nyght, so hateth she derknesse.

Hire chere is pleynly sprad in the brightnesse
Of the sonne, for ther yt wol unclose.
Allas, that I ne had Englyssh, ryme or prose,
Suffisant this flour to preyse aryght!
But helpeth, ye that han konnyng and myght,
Ye lovers that kan make of sentement;
In this cas oghte ye be diligent
To forthren me somwhat in my labour,
Whethir ye ben with the leef or with the flour.
For wel I wot that ye han her-biforn
Of makyng ropen, and lad awey the corn,
And I come after, glenyng here and there,
And am ful glad yf I may fynde an ere
Of any goodly word that ye han left.
And thogh it happen me rehercen eft
That ye han in your fresshe songes sayd,
Forbereth me, and beth nat evele apayd,
Syn that ye see I do yt in the honour
Of love, and eke in service of the flour

Whom that I serve as I have wit or myght.
She is the clernesse and the verray lyght
That in this derke world me wynt and ledeth.
The hert in-with my sorwfull brest yow dredeth
And loveth so sore that ye ben verrayly
The maistresse of my wit, and nothing I.
My word, my werk ys knyt so in youre bond
That, as an harpe obeieth to the hond
And maketh it soune after his fyngerynge,
Ryght so mowe ye oute of myn herte bringe
Swich vois, ryght as yow lyst, to laughe or pleyne.
Be ye my gide and lady sovereyne!
As to myn erthly god to yow I calle,
Bothe in this werk and in my sorwes alle.

    But wherfore that I spak, to yive credence
To olde stories and doon hem reverence,
And that men mosten more thyng beleve
Then men may seen at eye, or elles preve –
That shal I seyn, whanne that I see my tyme;
I may not al at-ones speke in ryme.
My besy gost, that thursteth alwey newe
To seen this flour so yong, so fressh of hewe,
Constreyned me with so gledy desir
That in myn herte I feele yet the fir
That made me to ryse er yt were day –
And this was now the firste morwe of May –
With dredful hert and glad devocioun,
For to ben at the resureccioun

Of this flour, whan that yt shulde unclose
Agayn the sonne, that roos as red as rose,
That in the brest was of the beste, that day,
That Agenores doghtre ladde away.
And doun on knes anoon-ryght I me sette,
And, as I koude, this fresshe flour I grette,
Knelyng alwey, til it unclosed was,
Upon the smale, softe, swote gras,
That was with floures swote enbrouded al,
Of swich swetnesse and swich odour overal,
That, for to speke of gomme, or herbe, or tree,
Comparisoun may noon ymaked bee;
For yt surmounteth pleynly alle odoures,
And of riche beaute alle floures.

THE COMPLAINT UNTO PITY

Pite, that I have sought so yore agoo
With herte soore and ful of besy peyne,
That in this world was never wight so woo
Withoute deth – and yf I shal not feyne,
My purpos was to Pite to compleyne
Upon the crueltee and tirannye
Of Love, that for my trouthe doth me dye.

And when that I, be lengthe of certeyne yeres,
Had evere in oon a tyme sought to speke,
To Pitee ran I al bespreynt with teres
To prayen hir on Cruelte me awreke.
But er I myghte with any word outbreke
Or tellen any of my peynes smerte,
I fond hir ded, and buried in an herte.

Adoun I fel when that I saugh the herse,
Ded as a ston while that the swogh me laste;
But up I roos with colour ful dyverse
And pitously on hir myn eyen I caste,
And ner the corps I gan to presen faste,
And for the soule I shop me for to preye.
I was but lorn, ther was no more to seye.

Thus am I slayn sith that Pite is ded.
Allas, that day, that ever hyt shulde falle.
What maner man dar now hold up his hed?
To whom shal any sorwful herte calle?
Now Cruelte hath cast to slee us alle,
In ydel hope, folk redeless of peyne,
Syth she is ded, to whom shul we compleyne?

But yet encreseth me this wonder newe,
That no wight woot that she is ded, but I –
So many men as in her tyme hir knewe –
And yet she dyed not so sodeynly,
For I have sought hir ever ful besely
Sith first I hadde wit or mannes mynde,
But she was ded er that I koude hir fynde.

Aboute hir herse there stoden lustely,
Withouten any woo as thoughte me,
Bounte parfyt, wel armed and richely,
And fresshe Beaute, Lust, and Jolyte,
Assured Maner, Youthe, and Honeste,
Wisdom, Estaat, Drede, and Governaunce,
Confedred both by bonde and alliaunce.

A compleynt had I, writen in myn hond,
For to have put to Pite as a bille;
But when I al this companye ther fond,
That rather wolden al my cause spille
Then do me help, I held my pleynte stille,
For to that folk, withouten any fayle,
Withoute Pitee ther may no bille availe.

Then leve I al these vertues, sauf Pite,
Kepynge the corps as ye have herd me seyn,
Confedered alle by bond of Cruelte
And ben assented when I shal be sleyn.
And I have put my complaynt up ageyn,
For to my foes my bille I dar not shewe,
Th'effect of which seith thus, in wordes fewe:

The Bill of Complaint

Humblest of herte, highest of reverence,
Benygne flour, coroune of vertues alle,
Sheweth unto youre rial excellence
Youre servaunt, yf I durste me so calle,
Hys mortal harm in which he is yfalle,
And noght al oonly for his evel fare,
But for your renoun, as he shal declare.

Hit stondeth thus: your contraire, Crueltee,
Allyed is ayenst your regalye,
Under colour of womanly Beaute –
For men shulde not, lo, knowe hir tirannye –
With Bounte, Gentilesse, and Curtesye,
And hath depryved yow now of your place
That hyghte 'Beaute apertenant to Grace.'

For kyndely by youre herytage ryght
Ye ben annexed ever unto Bounte;
And verrayly ye oughte do youre myght
To helpe Trouthe in his adversyte.
Ye be also the corowne of Beaute,
And certes yf ye wanten in these tweyne,
The world is lore; ther is no more to seyne.

Eke what availeth Maner and Gentilesse
Withoute yow, benygne creature?
Shal Cruelte be your governeresse?
Allas, what herte may hyt longe endure?
Wherfore, but ye the rather take cure
To breke that perilouse alliaunce,
Ye sleen hem that ben in your obeisaunce.

And further over yf ye suffre this,
Youre renoun ys fordoo than in a throwe;
Ther shal no man wite well what Pite is.
Allas, that your renoun is falle so lowe!
Ye be than fro youre heritage ythrowe
By Cruelte that occupieth youre place,
And we despeyred that seken to your grace.

Have mercy on me, thow Herenus quene,
That yow have sought so tendirly and yore;
Let som strem of youre lyght on me be sene
That love and drede yow ever lenger the more;
For sothly for to seyne I bere the soore,
And though I be not konnynge for to pleyne,
For Goddis love have mercy on my peyne.

My peyne is this, that what so I desire
That have I not, ne nothing lyk therto;
And ever setteth Desir myn hert on fire.
Eke on that other syde where so I goo,
What maner thing that may encrese my woo,
That have I redy, unsoght, everywhere;
Me lakketh but my deth and than my bere.

What nedeth to shewe parcel of my peyne?
Syth every woo that herte may bethynke
I suffre and yet I dar not to yow pleyne;
For wel I wot although I wake or wynke,
Ye rekke not whether I flete or synke.
But natheles yet my trouthe I shal sustene
Unto my deth, and that shal wel be sene.

This is to seyne I wol be youres evere,
Though ye me slee by Crueltee your foo,
Algate my spirit shal never dissevere
Fro youre servise for any peyne or woo.
Sith ye be ded – allas that hyt is soo –
Thus for your deth I may wel wepe and pleyne
With herte sore and ful of besy peyne.

GLOSSARY

The General Prologue

p.7   soote – sweet
         priketh – incites
         corages – hearts
         sondry londes – distant shrines

The Prioresse, the Knight and the Squire

p.9   fetisly – elegantly
         raughte – reached
         sikerly – truly
         tretys – well-formed
p.11   werre – war
         ferre – further
         eek – also
         lystes – duels
         gay – richly dressed
p.12   gypon – tunic
         habergeon – coat of mail
         delyvere – agile
         chyvachie – cavalry
         flotynge – piping

The Monk

p.13   streit – strict

118

swynken – work
prikasour – horseman
p.14   purfiled – lined
grys – fur
stepe – bright
forpyned – tormented

The Friar

p.15   lymytour – licensed to beg
yshryve – confessed
p.16   yeddynges – recitations
lazar – leper
poraille – poor people
rage – flirt

The Wife of Bath

p.18   scathe – a pity
p.19   targe – shield
carpe – chatter

The Reeve's Tale

p.20   melle – mill
panade – cutlass
poppere – dagger
piled – bald
market-betere – bully
p.21   ynorissed – raised, bred
gyte – gown

smoterlich – sullied
hoker – disdain
nortelrie – education
page – boy
p.22   catel – property
mesuage – house and contents
hye – nobly
sokene – monopoly
in a stounde – once
stal – stole
fare – a fuss
tare – weed
cracketh boost – blustered
p.23   Testif – testy
reve – rob
swayn – servant
wanges – teeth
p.24   hopur – hopper (of the mill)
ille – poor
nycetee – foolishness
blere – trick
crekes – tricks
p.25   levesel – arbour
banes – bones
unthank – curses
p.26   capul – horse
lathe – barn
Ilhayl – bad luck
fonne – fool

The Franklin's Tale

p.35   dide his payne – made an effort
       emprise – enterprise
       unnethes – hardly
       pryvely – secretly
       kithe – show
       for shame of his degree – out of regard for his
            rank
p.36   As in my gilt – through my fault
       complexioun – temperament
       wreken – avenged
p.37   kan – has skill in
       behight – promised
p.38   stynten of – leave
       siketh – became ill
       duren – continue
p.39   purveiaunce – foresight
       In ydel – in vain
p.40   yfostred – nourished
       chiertee – affection
p.41   But if – unless
p.42   beste farynge – most handsome
       biwreye – reveal
p.43   worshipe – good reputation
       gerdon – reward
       reweth – have pity
p.44   aleyes – garden paths
p.45   breyde – awoke

122

123

From Troilus and Criseyde

126

From the Legend of Good Women

127